DIMENSIONS
of the
MODERN
PRESIDENCY

DIMENSIONS
of the
MODERN
PRESIDENCY

Edward N. Kearny, Editor
Western Kentucky University

The Forum Press, Inc.
Arlington Heights, Illinois 60004

To my parents, Mr. and Mrs. E. N. Kearny, Jr.

Published simultaneously in Canada

Printed in the United States of America

82 83 84 85 86CB 9 8 7 6 5 4 3 2

Library of Congress Catalog Card Number: 80-68461

ISBN: 0-88273-268-4

Cover Design by Mel Lovings

Contents

Ronald Reagan and his running mate George Bush are joined by former President Gerald Ford at the close of the 1980 Republican Convention. *(Wide World Photos)*

Preface

This book contains eleven original essays on the *Dimensions of the Modern Presidency*. The authors, although dealing with sophisticated scholarly material, have made a special effort to write in a clear understandable way for the undergraduate reader. The essays do not assume a high level of prior knowledge by the student. Specialized terminology has been scrupulously avoided. Generalizations and concepts are carefully explained.

This book is designed to provide a new kind of supplementary reading for courses on the American presidency and introductory American government courses. While supplementary readings for courses on the presidency are often highly specialized, the essays in this volume are much more general in scope. Moreover, supplementary readers are often collections of reprinted and dated material, while the essays presented here are original and more current. For these reasons, this book should fill a need for teachers of undergraduate courses on the presidency.

The collection is also designed to be useful in introductory American government courses. The essays explore ten standard areas of the field *from a presidential perspective*. Because of the President's central position in the governmental system, this perspective throws considerable light on all facets of American government and politics, and does so in a highly stimulating fashion.

I am grateful to the contributors for their diligent work and their responsiveness to editorial suggestions. I also wish to express my appreciation to the political scientists who read the essays in their areas of interest and offered their comments: Professors Elbert T. Dubose of Lamar University, James Foster of Columbus College, Charles W. Hill of Roanoke College, James Klonoski of the University of Oregon, and John Parker of Western Kentucky University. Responsibility for the "final product," however, rests with the individual contributors and the editor. I also wish to express my appreciation to Dr. W. A. Welsh, president of Forum Press, for his support and assistance.

Edward N. Kearny
Editor

Introduction: The Presidency in the 1980s

Norman Thomas

University of Cincinnati

Perhaps two of the most commonly held expectations of a successful President are that he will "lead the people" and "run the government." This book is divided into two major parts. Each contains five essays which carefully examine the problems and complexities facing Presidents as they try to meet these two expectations.

Professor Thomas, in the introductory essay which follows, examines broad general factors which affect both the President's relationship to the people and his relationship to the government. One set of factors includes the strengths and weaknesses of the presidency as a political institution. Thomas traces its rapid expansion in size and prestige in the wake of the Great Depression and World War II. He then describes how the prestige and power of the office suffered substantial setbacks as a result of the adverse national reaction to the Vietnam War and the Watergate scandals.

Thomas demonstrates how changes in the prestige and power of the institution of the presidency have a profound effect on the prospects of any incumbent President regardless of his personal characteristics. Yet Thomas also maintains that the personal characteristics of a President constitute a second set of factors which play an important role in determining his problems and prospects. Is the

1

President a skilled politician who can bargain effectively with the "insiders" who hold political power in Washington and elsewhere? Is his general personality style suited or unsuited to the demands of the modern presidency? After examining these questions, Thomas warns that the modern presidency may be harmed most by expecting too much from it. Inflated promises by Presidents and presidential candidates encourage unrealistic expectations on the part of the people. Conversely, such unrealistic popular expectations encourage Presidents to make inflated promises. Both are likely to lead to further disillusionment with our system of free government when performance falls short of unreachable expectations.

ENK

President Jimmy Carter's problems during his fourth year in office provide a point of departure for our consideration of the presidency in the 1980s. As the new decade began, problems of crisis or near crisis dimensions persisted in both foreign and domestic policy areas. Virulent inflation, potential energy shortages, growing dependence on imported oil, and rising American-Soviet tensions dominated the threatening political atmosphere in which Carter campaigned for reelection.

There were serious public doubts about the capacity of the nation's political institutions—Congress, the presidency, and the federal bureaucracy—to respond effectively to crucial challenges. Many people, and all of Mr. Carter's challengers for the presidency, questioned his ability to provide the leadership which would make those institutions more effective.

Political analysts have offered several explanations for the difficulties in which President Carter found himself. Their formulations seem to cluster around two central themes; one institutional, the other personal. The institutional explanation suggests that Carter has the misfortune to be in office at a time when the presidency has been gravely weakened by a resurgent Congress which rushed to restore constitutional parity with the President in the wake of Vietnam and Watergate. The cycle of presidential ascendancy which began with the New Deal ended in the early 1970s and, it is argued, Congress has reasserted itself.

Another line of institutional reasoning holds that structural features and long-term trends in the political system are primarily responsible for Carter's inability to persuade Congress to respond to his initiatives and for the resulting weakness in his popular support. According to this view, the constitutional separation of powers with its accompanying checks and balances, the parochial orientation of Congress and most of its members, the weakness of our national political parties and the proliferation of interest groups combine to make it impossible for any President to govern the nation effectively.

The second major school of thought seeks the explanation of President Carter's troubles in his personal characteristics. He has been unable to lead Congress and gain command of the nation's pressing problems, it is argued, because he has not adapted well to the demands of the many roles that the President must fill. Elected as an "outsider" who campaigned against the "Washington Establishment," Carter has also drawn sharp criticisms for his failure to reach an accommodation with that establishment. Without such an accommodation, the argument continues, no President can hope to accomplish his policy goals. President Carter's personality and his leadership style are cited as the principal reasons for his inability to adapt well to various presidential roles or to make the necessary accommodations with the national policymaking system.

Undoubtedly there is some measure of validity in both of these approaches. But neither approach, taken singly, can serve as a satisfactory basis for explaining the condition of the presidency as the United States enters the 1980s. Together, however, they can provide a basis for analyzing presidential power and its limitations and for assessing the capacity of the presidency to meet the challenges of the 1980s. Let us first look at the office from an institutional perspective.

THE OFFICE: IMPERIAL OR CRIPPLED?

As the American presidency enters the 1980s, it presents us with something of a paradox. On the one hand it is rightfully viewed as the most powerful elective office in the world and people look upon the President as the symbolic personification of the nation. At home and abroad, the President is expected to speak for the United States and to provide leadership that solves the problem that it faces. On the other hand, the powers of the office have been curtailed and its stature has diminished sharply in the last decade. The ability of individual Presidents to solve intractable social, economic, and foreign-policy problems is clearly limited and the presidency no longer seems able to counterbalance the centrifugal forces in American political life as it did not too long ago. There is evidence to support both sides of this apparent paradox surrounding the presidential office.

Presidential power has expanded manyfold since 1933. Immediately following his inauguration, President Franklin D. Roosevelt moved on the basis of constitutional prerogatives and existing statutory delegations of authority to mobilize an attack on the Great Depression. Throughout the Roosevelt administration, Congress made sweeping delegations of authority to the President and to executive departments and agencies as the United States coped first with economic collapse and then with a global war. During that period the nation developed an extensive dependence on the executive branch of the national government to solve its problems.

In the years that followed World War II, Presidents continued and expanded Roosevelt's practice of developing and submitting comprehensive legislative proposals to Congress. Presidential direction of foreign and military policy was taken for granted and bipartisan support of the administration in office became the norm. Although Congress clearly had constitutional and political independence from the presidency, most of the time it chose not to assert itself. To the extent that there were coherent national policies which were related to each other, that integration was provided by the presidency.

The President also served as the strongest and most visible link between the public and the national government. The American people began a lengthy love affair with the presidency and their Presidents. The advent of mass communications—national magazines and newspapers and, most importantly, television—enabled Presidents to reach the people on an unprecedentedly broad scale. And the people responded with affection for Presidents and their families and almost reverential support for the presidency. The constant focus of the media on the President, the glorification of presidential government by journalists and scholars as the embodiment of democracy, and the willingness of many congressional and other political leaders to defer to presidential judgment, produced in the public a grossly exaggerated view of the capabilities of the presidency and exaggerated expectations of presidential performance. Presidents themselves contributed to the development of this unrealistic view of the presidency by making exaggerated promises and claims in their campaigns for office.

In addition to the expansion of both formal presidential powers (based on legal authority) and informal powers (based on popular support) there occurred a striking transformation in the structure of the presidency. From what was a loose collection of a few dozen clerical personnel and a handful of presidential assistants during the Hoover administration, the presidency has become a large, complex bureaucracy with many of the problems that are associated with such organizations.

The original rationale for the creation of an "institution-alized" presidency was to provide the President with sufficient staff assistance to enable him to meet his expanded responsibilities. "The President needs help," stated the 1937 report of the President's Committee on Administrative Management. Two years later Congress responded by establishing the Executive Office of the President and transferring the Bureau of the Budget (BOB) from the Treasury Department to the Executive Office. BOB, which became the Office of Management and Budget (OMB) in 1970, has been one of the President's key staff units. Other staff offices and units have been added to the Executive Office since 1939 as the President has acquired important new responsibilities and as Presidents have sought to improve their relations with Congress and interest groups and to enhance their control over the federal bureaucracy. Today, the major components of the Executive Office include the White House staff, OMB, the National Security Council and its staff, the Council of Economic Advisers and its staff, the Domestic Policy Staff, the press office, and liaison offices to handle relations with Congress and with interest groups and other constituencies. In 1980, President Carter had 417 persons serving on the White House staff as compared with 48 in 1944 or 263 in 1963.

There is little disagreement that the President needs ample staff support in order to fill his legislative and administrative responsibilities, to evaluate the consequences of various policies and programs, and to analyze long-range problems and develop plans for dealing with them. However, by 1970 what Thomas Cronin refers to as the "swelling of the presidency" became a serious problem. Presidents, especially Johnson and Nixon, isolated themselves within their overgrown bureaucracies and were protected from criticism and shielded from negative information by loyal aides. The layers of presidential assistants also insulated Presidents from much direct contact with cabinet members and with congressional leaders. Presidents increasingly made their decisions surrounded by loyalists and sycophants who reinforced the values and prejudices of their chiefs and screened out hardheaded but constructively critical analysis.

Moreover, as Presidents faltered in their efforts to control cabinet members and their departments, they assigned some of the tasks of operating the departments to their staff aides and offices. However, "salvation by staff" proved unsatisfactory. The involvement of presidential staff members in the management of the bureaucracy reduced their ability to perform the essential function of staff which is to objectively analyze problems and evaluate courses of action from a variety of perspectives.

The almost continual growth of presidential power beginning in the 1930s, the public's fascination with the presidency, the adulation of individual Presidents, exaggerated expectations of presidential performance and the development of a swollen presidential establishment combined to produce what Arthur Schlesinger called the "imperial presidency." The involvement of the United States in an extended war in Vietnam as a result of a series of presidential decisions extending as far back as 1954, the absence of formal congressional authorization of that war, and widespread popular opposition to the war in the late 1960s led to an attack on the imperial presidency. Scholars such as Schlesinger and George Reedy (who had served as Johnson's press secretary) argued that presidential power had been expanded dangerously beyond its constitutional boundaries. They charged that presidential power had been grossly abused. Ironically, many critics of the imperial presidency had been among the strongest advocates of a strong presidency during the 1950s and early 1960s.

The decline of the imperial presidency began with its overextension in Vietnam and in the resultant antiwar movement in the United States. However, its undoing did not come about until the Watergate scandal led to the resignation of President Richard Nixon in 1974. Shortly after his landslide reelection victory in 1972, Nixon became embroiled in efforts by key White House staff persons to cover up the relationship between the White House and the agents of the Committee to Reelect the President who were caught breaking into Democratic National Committee headquarters, located in the Watergate Hotel in Washington, on June 17, 1972. As various legislative and judicial investigations of Watergate proceeded, Nixon's involvement in the cover-up became increasingly manifest. Eventually almost all of his energy was devoted to the matter. Finally, after the House Judiciary Committee approved three impeachment charges against Nixon, he resigned on August 8, 1974.

As the Watergate affair unfolded and Nixon's position weakened, Congress initiated a series of steps designed to curb the presidency:

1) In 1973 it made the President's appointments to the directorship and deputy directorship of OMB subject to confirmation by the Senate. This was in response to Nixon's actions that had made OMB a more politically oriented agency.

2) In the same year Congress refused to renew the President's authority, originally granted in 1939, to propose executive branch reorganization plans to Congress which then had sixty days in which to reject them. In 1977, Congress renewed the reorganization power for President Carter but made it subject to certain restraints.

3) Also in 1973, Congress passed the War Powers Resolution over Nixon's veto. That legislation requires that the President consult with Congress prior to committing military forces to action abroad. It further requires that the President report such commitments to Congress in writing within forty-eight hours and if Congress does not authorize the commitment within sixty days, it must be terminated.

4) The Impoundment Control Act of 1974 sharply restricted presidential power to return appropriated funds to the Treasury. Nixon had used that authority, which was originally given to the President to help prevent waste, as a means of substituting his spending priorities for those of Congress. (In 1973 alone, for example, Nixon impounded $18 billion).

5) In the National Emergencies Act of 1976, Congress terminated several states of emergency extending as far back as 1933. Those states of emergency were the basis of ex-

tensive presidential powers. The act also established procedures for congressional review of the declaration of future emergencies and of presidential use of emergency powers.

In addition to these specific steps, Congress has expanded its use of the congressional veto, a procedure which enables it to prevent a President or his administration from acting on the basis of existing statutory authority. In instituting the congressional veto, Congress provides in a statute that certain actions may be disallowed either by a concurrent resolution of Congress, or a resolution of either house, or by one or more designated committees. Presidents have objected strenuously to the congressional veto even though they have signed bills authorizing it.

It is not possible to determine the extent to which these specific actions that Congress took during the 1970s amount to a major curtailment of presidential authority. But the symbolic significance of the actions cannot be denied. Congress clearly asserted its determination to keep Presidents under closer rein. And Presidents Ford and Carter have felt the pull of those reins. For example, in 1975, Ford felt compelled to ask Congress for special authority to provide $25 million in assistance to the pro-Western faction in the Angolan civil conflict even though he had general authority to take such action. Congress refused the request and no aid was sent. Carter has felt congressional resistance to his initiatives in all major policy areas almost from the outset of his administration.

Both Ford and Carter took steps while in office to "demystify" and "de-imperialize" the presidency. They downplayed much of the pomp and ceremony that surround the office and consciously tried to appear more human and approachable. Shortly after taking office, Ford told an audience that he was "a Ford and not a Lincoln." Carter appeared on television for a fireside chat early in his first year wearing a cardigan sweater. These and similar efforts to adopt a common touch did not meet with full approval, however, as both men were criticized on occasion for not being sufficiently "presidential." Apparently the public retains considerable esteem for the presidency even though it may delight in seeing a self-made "common man" in the White House. President Carter apparently recognized that there is substantial strength in public expectations that the President will perform the ceremonial aspects of his role willingly and with dignity, for by his fourth year in office he had abandoned many of his early symbolic attempts to demonstrate his common touch. The assertion is sometimes made that the presidency has been dangerously crippled by the congressional resurgence of the 1970s and by the conscious efforts of Presidents Ford and Carter to place it on a more human and less elevated plane. A related line of institutional analysis holds that while these recent factors have undoubtedly been important in reducing the power of the presidency, other factors of a more basic and long-term nature have been more important.

According to this point of view, the constitutional separation of powers, the local orientation of Congress, and the fragmentation of congressional leadership are key features of the governmental structure that make it very difficult for any President to provide leadership that results in coherent policies which will solve the nation's problems. The framers of the Constitution feared both unrestrained popular majorities and the abuse of governmental authority so they created a government in which separate legislative, executive, and judicial institutions would share power. The system was deliberately designed to govern on the basis of a national consensus. A basic premise underlying the constitutional system is that no action is preferable to hasty, ill-considered action taken without widespread popular support. Thus, we should not be surprised that President Carter's comprehensive energy proposals were exhaustively considered and drained of much of their substantive impact by Congress. The national government is functioning much as it was designed to do.

As for Congress, its preoccupation with the protection and enhancement of local interests and its apparent lack of concern with the national interest is also in conformity with the original design. The framers had little conception of a great national legislature passing bills that would have worldwide impact. They did envision a body that would be responsive to state and regional interests and that would reflect the concerns of the people. To a considerable extent, Congress still meets those expectations.

The local orientation of Congress is a function of the preoccupation of its members with being reelected and their dependence for reelection on constituency-based forces. Neither the President, national party organizations, nor congressional party leaders have control over a member's reelection. According to David Mayhew, the behavior of individual members and much of the institutional behavior of Congress is explainable by the "electoral connection" with constituencies. The fragmentation of power and the weakness of party leadership in Congress is further enhanced by the committee system, the proliferation of subcommittees, and the selection of committee and subcommittee leaders according to the norm of seniority. Presidents are unable to influence the fragmented structure of power in Congress and often they have great difficulty finding anyone who can negotiate with them on behalf of Congress. The formation of a sustained winning congressional coalition has become almost impossible in the face of constituency and group strength and party weakness among the members. Instead, Presidents have to try to fashion a new majority for every important legislative proposal. Even such fleeting majorities are hard to obtain because of the multiplicity of issues and interests that must be accommodated and the absence of power brokers in Congress with the ability to arrange settlements. As one Washington correspondent recently observed, it has become extremely difficult (for the President) to get things done. The lack of institutional leadership capability in Congress is matched by the President's inability to command or create congressional majorities.

Party weakness in Congress is paralleled by party weakness in the electorate as there has been a marked decline in partisan identification and a rise in the proportion of independent voters since 1964. In its study of the 1978 congressional election, the University of Michigan's Center for Political Studies found that 39 percent of a national sample survey identified themselves as Democrats, 21 percent as Republicans and 37 percent as independents. (In 1964 the figures were 51 percent, 24 percent, and 23 percent, respectively.) The steady decline in public support for the parties has further weakened their traditionally limited ability to mobilize interests and convert them into electoral and congressional majorities. At the same time, there has been a proliferation of new groups representing hitherto unorganized interests such as recipients of social services, the poor, state and local governments, public employees, consumers, environmentalists, the general public interest, and a variety of militant single-issue groups typified by the pro and antiabortion forces.

Traditionally in democracies political parties have performed the key function of gathering the demands of voters and interest groups and converting them into policy proposals. But American parties are now so weak that they can no longer perform the task satisfactorily—if indeed they ever did. The political system has an excess of interest groups and of popular participation through nonparty and nonelectoral channels. These forces make it extremely difficult for a President to overcome the obstacles to governmental action presented by the constitutional separation of powers. Given the multiplicity of problems that seemingly resist solutions, it is difficult to see how any President can govern effectively under such conditions. It has been suggested with increasing frequency that the key question in analyzing American politics should not be "who governs?", but "does anybody govern?"

Although the imperial presidency is temporarily out of favor, it is the only political institution capable of overcoming the atomization of the political system. The fragmentation of power in contemporary American politics through the proliferation of strong interest and issue groups and party weakness, the degeneration of elections into popularity contests to be won by candidates with the best organizations of professional public relations people and market researchers, and the immobilization of a Congress that has become a vehicle for the defense and promotion of local interests seems to some observers almost to ensure that the next major national crisis will bring a restoration of the imperial presidency.

While I do not subscribe fully to such a pessimistic assessment of the presidential office and of our national political system, it gives me cause for concern. The problem, as I view it, is not whether the presidency is too strong or too weak in the short run, but whether the governmental structure created by the Constitution and the political system that operates it are "adequate to the exigencies of the union." (This phrase was used by the Annapolis Convention of 1786 when it recommended that a convention be held to consider revisions in the Articles of Confederation.) If the only way that modern American government can deal effectively with the complex challenges of the late twentieth century is through reliance on increased presidential power, then we must question its long-term adequacy.

THE MAN: INSIDER OR OUTSIDER?

The second major approach to understanding the presidency lies through the study of presidential personality. Accepting institutional and other long-term factors as given, this school of thought seeks to explain presidential performance in terms of the character, attitudes, and behavior patterns of individual Presidents. The purpose of personality-centered analyses is to prescribe how a President should act in order to accomplish his objectives. Presidential failures can thus be explained as failures to follow the prescriptions offered.

The dominant prescriptive model for leadership employed by students of the presidency is that developed by Richard Neustadt in his book *Presidential Power*. Neustadt argued that the formal powers of the presidency based on the Constitution and on statutory delegations are quite weak. In fact, they do little more than authorize the President to furnish services to other participants in the national policymaking establishment located in Washington. The restraints imposed on the President by other "Washingtonians" are so extensive that he has almost no power to command. If the President is to transcend the limits of his constitutional "clerkship," he must do so through the exercise of skilled leadership. The principal leadership skill is persuasion. According to Neustadt, presidential power is the power to persuade and the power to persuade depends on bargaining. In order to gain power the President must know how to bargain.

The key to successful presidential bargaining, Neustadt argues, lies in sensitivity to personal power. The President must be sensitive to his power stakes and the power stakes of those whom he seeks to persuade. He must be able to turn the self-interest of other power holders to his advantage by convincing them that it is to their advantage to do what he wants. In addition, he needs to maintain his reputation as a skilled leader among those whom he must persuade. To the extent that the President is able to win other power holders to his cause, the national government will function effectively.

By implication Presidents must work within the framework of the national policymaking establishment (the Washington community). They cannot expect to be effective persuaders if they do not understand the workings of the establishment, if they resist its norms, or if they attempt to overcome it by appeals for popular support.

In terms of Neustadt's model, Jimmy Carter's difficulties are due largely to his refusal or inability to learn the ways of the Washingtonians and to bargain with them in terms of their political self-interest. Elected as an outsider on an anti-Washington platform, Carter has maintained that stance in office. Rather than adapt to the expectations of the Washingtonians he has attempted to pressure them to conform to his mode of operation. Indeed, when he has encountered resistance from Congress, the bureaucracy, and national interest groups, he has often responded with an attack on the offending individuals and institutions and with criticism of Washington as an "island" isolated from the mainstream of the nation's economic and social life. He has called upon the public to support him in his struggle with self-serving politicians, bureaucrats, and interests. Although this approach may play well on the campaign trail, it is argued, it is hardly the way to get things done in Washington.

Carter's difficulties in developing effective policy leadership also stem from his preference for a rational-comprehensive approach to problems rather than on the incremental (piecemeal) bargaining that the political system requires. Instead of making the pragmatic compromises needed to build congressional majorities to pass his proposals, Carter attempts to prevail by logical analysis and the weight of the evidence. However, cost-benefit analysis has never been very persuasive in Washington.

Trained as an engineer, Carter has not understood that rationality in national policy politics is determined on the basis of power stakes and political self-interest. According to Aaron Wildavsky, Carter is "more of a planner than a politician." He places dominant emphasis on the form rather than the substance of policies and is more concerned with the uniformity, predictability, and comprehensiveness of policies than with their content. The danger for President Carter, says Wildavsky, "is not that he will support unpopular *policies*, but that he will persevere with inappropriate procedures." Carter's rational-comprehensive view of policymaking is what has driven him to assume the role of chief national spokesman for the public interest which he determines through direct contact with the people (as in his "town meetings" and national telephone answer programs). It is a deficient tactic because it has led him to reject bargaining with interest groups and their congressional allies over policy. Ultimately, it is an untenable approach because "interests do differ, because the price of agreement is likely to be vagueness, and because administration involves altering ends by changing means."

The reasons why Carter has refused to drop the posture of the outsider and play the policymaking game by Washington's rules are not provided by Wildavsky nor to be found in Neustadt. Wildavsky hints that Carter's engineering background may offer a partial explanation (after all Hoover was an engineer) but being an engineer does not necessarily prevent one from becoming a pragmatic politician. Neustadt would probably take Carter's refusal to bargain in terms of his power stakes as evidence of unsuitability for the job.

A different explanation can be suggested on the basis of James David Barber's theory of presidential leadership based on personality development. Character is the core of Barber's theory. He defines character as "the way the President orients himself toward life." It is based on two behavioral dimensions; activity-passivity and positive-negative attitude or feeling toward one's activity. There are four basic character types; active-positive, active-negative, passive-positive, and passive-negative. They are accompanied by behavior which is adaptive, compulsive, compliant, and obligatory or duty-bound respectively.

Using Barber's classification scheme, Carter's behavior often appears to be that of an active-negative.* He clearly is an active President, but he has been unable to adapt to all of the demands and expectations of the President's many roles or to the Washington policymaking process. Carter's determined pursuit of the presidency, his rigid defense of his positions, his unyielding and unquestioning loyalty to subordinates who embarrassed him, *e.g.,* former Budget Director Bert Lance, his insistence on filling key staff positions with associates from Georgia politics whose knowledge of Washington politics and of substantive policies was limited and his compulsive fixation on the instrumental and

---

*Shortly after Carter was elected, Barber assessed him as a probable active-positive, but noted signs of compulsiveness that could indicate an active-negative character (Barber, 1977, Chapter 16).

technological aspects of policymaking are indicative of an active-negative character. According to Barber, the active-negative has a "perfectionistic conscience" that is reflected in two themes, a denial of self-gratification and concern with self-control, and a political style that is "persistent and emphatic." The self-esteem of an active-negative is built on holding the presidency. Anyone who threatens that self-esteem provokes the President to a rigidity that is ultimately self-destructive.

Whether Carter's behavior matches this description or whether it is more accurately characterized by the well-adjusted, self-confident flexibility of an active-positive is not readily apparent. A case can be made for Carter as an active-positive. For example, he skillfully brokered the delicate personal negotiations between Israeli Premier Begin and Egyptian President Sadat and brought the two nations to a peace treaty; he did not panic when challenged by Edward Kennedy for the 1980 Democratic nomination even though the senator seemed at the time to be more charismatic and popular than the President; and his record of legislative successes, which is much greater than his detractors concede, indicates that he possesses considerable political skill and adaptability.

If nothing else, the ambiguity over Carter's placement in the Barber typology is indicative of its imprecise categories and of the difficulty of applying personality-centered explanations of presidential performance. Carter is a complex individual who neither conforms to the dominant political science model (derived from Neustadt) of a power-maximizing strong President nor readily fits one of Barber's character types. The Carter presidency, in its complexity and unpredictability, clearly demonstrates the limits of analyses based solely on the personal style of the President.

CONCLUSION: HELPING THE TROUBLED PRESIDENCY

Regardless of his personal style, Ronald Reagan, who was inaugurated on January 20, 1981 confronts the difficult task of attempting to govern the nation under the constitutional structure of separate institutions sharing powers. The question that the American people face is whether the presidency can provide the leadership to build sustained public support for actions to solve national problems. A related question is whether Congress will develop the institutional leadership that will make it an independent but not antagonistic counterweight to the presidency.

Are these realistic demands to make of our government? Certainly the institutional arrangements, the weakness of political parties, and the domination of policymaking by interest groups present substantial challenges to the American republic that has operated under its present Constitution since 1789. Assuming that the American people are not about to abandon the Constitution for, say, parliamentary government, what can be done to strengthen the troubled governmental institutions and processes for making national policy that function under it? More particularly, can we restore to the presidency the effectiveness that it seemingly had from the 1930s to the 1960s?

The answers to such questions are by no means clear and definitive, but they suggest more realistic perceptions of government and Presidents and what they can do. We need to realize that the election of a new President, however dynamic and inspiring he may seem, does not produce quick and easy solutions to the nation's problems. Nor do the institutional and political impediments to successful presidential leadership suddenly vanish. Over-inflated promises by candidates should be viewed with caution for they are likely to lead to further popular disillusionment with our system of free government when presidential performance falls short of expectations. A smaller and more flexible conception of the presidency and its capabilities is in order. As David Broder, nationally syndicated columnist for the Washington Post, recently observed, "the failures that have weakened the Presidency. . .have resulted from over-reaching, not under-achieving." If we bear this point in mind as we enter the 1980s, the presidency should serve the nation more effectively than it did in the 1970s.

Suggested Readings

Barber, James David, *The Presidential Character: Predicting Performance in the White House,* 2nd ed. (Englewood Cliffs: Prentice-Hall, Inc., 1977). A controversial, personality-based theory of presidential behavior. It is interesting, well-written, and thought provoking.

Berman, Larry, *The Office of Management and Budget and the Presidency, 1921-1979* (Princeton: Princeton University Press, 1979). A comprehensive study of the President's primary institutional staff agency. The OMB's use and misuse by successive Presidents is the focus of the analysis.

Cronin, Thomas, E., *The State of the Presidency,* 2nd ed. (Boston: Little, Brown & Co., 1980). An analysis of the condition and the problems of the contemporary presidency.

Hess, Stephen, *Organizing the Presidency* (Washington: The Brookings Institution, 1976). An examination of the mode of operation and staffing arrangements by six Presidents from Franklin D. Roosevelt to Richard M. Nixon. The author suggests that we would benefit from a more collegial presidency.

King, Anthony, ed., *The New American Political System* (Washington: American Enterprise Institute for Public Policy Research, 1978). A collection of original essays by ten distinguished political scientists that assess the changes in the American political system during the 1960s and 1970s.

Neustadt, Richard E., *Presidential Power: The Politics of Leadership from FDR to Carter* (New York: John Wiley & Sons, Inc., 1980). Originally published in 1960, this book has provided the dominant conceptual model for political science analyses of the presidency.

Reedy, George E., *The Twilight of the Presidency* (New York: World, 1970). This book, by Lyndon B. Johnson's former press secretary, was one of the first "revisionist" attacks on the argument that the national interest requires a strong President.

Roositer, Clinton, *The American Presidency,* rev. ed. (New York: Harcourt, Brace & Co., 1960). A classic analysis cast in terms of the principal roles of the President.

Schlesinger, Arthur M., Jr., *The Imperial Presidency* (Boston: Houghton Mifflin Co., 1973). A scholarly analysis of the use and abuse of presidential power. In spite of his criticism of expanded presidential authority, the author cautions against excessive restraints on the presidency.

Wildavsky, Aaron, *The Politics of the Budgetary Process,* 3rd ed., (Boston: Little, Brown & Co., 1979). An insightful analysis of presidential, congressional, and agency roles and strategies in the budgetary process.

Jimmy Carter walks down Pennsylvania Avenue on his
Inauguration Day, January 1977. *(The White House)*

Part I

The President and the People

Almost everyone accepts the notion that one of the most important responsibilities a President has is to lead and inspire the American people. Yet very few people understand how extremely complicated this task is. The articles in this section describe the problems and complexities of a President's relationship to the people.

How does a President know what will inspire the American people? Polls often give him conflicting answers. Looking at some polls, the President might conclude that the people want a man who can rise above political "wheeling and dealing." But other polling data may suggest to him that the people also want a leader with exceptional political skills. Dozens of similar contradictions will demonstrate to him that the enormous quantity of polling data he possesses raises as many confusing questions as it answers.

If he is reasonably wise, the President will conclude that it is impossible to give a clear answer to the question, "What do the American people want?" Nevertheless, he will wish to reach out, to inspire, and to lead the people even if he cannot know precisely what they want.

The only way he can effectively reach out to all the people is through the news media. Although no President likes to admit it, he is hopeful that the media will serve as his megaphone, amplifying the message he wants to convey to millions of Americans.

19

Presidents are invariably disappointed, some more so than others, at the media's persistent unwillingness to be their megaphone. Newsmen want to know more about the President's failures as well as his successes. They want to talk to the President when he doesn't want to talk to them. Knowing the public is fascinated by his every step and stumble, the media is relentless in pursuing both. Presidents are eventually forced to conclude that the media is not a megaphone, but a double-edged sword which can help to bring conquest one day and defeat the next.

Dealing with the general public is difficult enough, but the President knows all too well that this is just the beginning. The American people love to organize themselves into interest groups for countless economic, social, and political purposes. Business groups, labor unions, farm organizations, ethnic groups, environmental groups, pro and antiabortion groups are only part of the total array of interest groups the American people have created.

When a citizen becomes active in an interest group, his or her political viewpoint is often narrowed and intensified at the same time. The interest group activist is likely to convey to the President, in one way or another, that if he is on the "wrong" side of the group's favored position, he will have a well-organized political foe to contend with regardless of his overall performance as President.

The President, therefore, is aware that in dealing with "the people" he must deal simultaneously with the whole (the general public) and many of its parts (organized interest groups). Maintaining his standing with the people, therefore, is a very difficult balancing act which must be performed on many levels at the same time.

"The bottom line" in any President's calculations during his first term is that if he is not renominated and reelected, he will lose his leadership connection with the American people altogether. To avoid this, he must win a vote of confidence in the *same* election year from two distinct constituencies: the relatively narrow ranks of his own party, and, if he is successful, the much broader ranks of the general electorate.

Interest groups which are powerful in his party will use his need for nomination to press their demands on him. He must take these demands seriously even if he believes them to be unwise in the broader context of the general election or of uniting the nation. For if he ignores them, party activists may cut him off from leadership of the American people by denying him the nomination.

So the President as a candidate in an election year finds that he must, in rapid succession, deal with the people in parts (his fellow partisans in fifty separate state contests) and then the people as a whole (the general electorate in the presidential election). He is forced once more to perform a very difficult balancing act in which he tries to appeal to different groupings of Americans in different arenas more or less at the same time.

The remarks above give the reader only a brief glimpse of the complexity of the President's relationship with the American people. The five essays in this section provide detailed accounts of what is involved when a President or a presidential hopeful sets out to lead and inspire his fellow countrymen.

President Lyndon Johnson meeting people, 1964. *(The National Archives)*

The President and Public Opinion

James Lea
University of Southern Mississippi

In recent years Americans have had reason for concern, curiously enough, about both the excesses and the deficiencies of presidential power. From the 1930s and 1940s when Franklin Roosevelt led the nation through the Great Depression and World War II to Richard Nixon's resignation in the 1970s as a result of unprecedented abuse of his powers, the presidency experienced a phenomenal increase in power.

The mid-to-late 1970s witnessed a post-Watergate reaction to the abuse of presidential powers which had become so broad that many observers began to refer to the White House establishment as the "imperial presidency." Congress reacted through specific legislation, such as that limiting the President's war and budgetary powers, and enacting campaign reforms aimed at making those seeking the office more accountable. In addition, there was a general reassertion of political-governmental authority not only by the Congress, but by the judiciary, the bureaucracy, the press, and others who wished to put the presidency in its proper place.

Some important voices were raised at mid-decade warning that too-extreme actions to control the imperial inclinations of the presidency might weaken the office. The leadership problems of the first two post-Watergate Presidents, Gerald Ford and Jimmy Carter, lent a sense of urgency to the concerns of those who feared the office was too greatly weakened to lead the nation effectively. Ex-President Ford asked, near the end of the decade, whether we did not now have an "imperiled President." It would seem that neither an "imperial" nor an "imperiled" presidency advances democratic ordering of the affairs of the American political community. Confronted with the paradoxical problem of, at one and the same time, controlling and reinforcing presidential authority, the nation has perhaps overemphasized laws and institutional checks and neglected what James Madison, the "father" of the United States Constitution, termed the "primary control," which is a "dependence on the people."

This "primary control" depends, of course, on the process of presidential nominations and elections. On an even more fundamental level, however, it depends on an effective public opinion process which induces Presidents to both *lead* and *follow* the popular will in a democratic fashion. This requires at least three things: (1) Presidents must be able to ascertain the public will; (2) Presidents must feel compelled both by their nature and political forces to "heed" or relate to this; and, (3) Presidents must have available to them effective, nonauthoritarian means of "public persuasion." We want to examine, in turn, each of these three aspects of the public opinion process. This democratic linkage of the American citizenry with their President may well offer the best hope for avoiding the extremes of excessive or insufficient power in the presidency. The effectiveness of this public opinion process is, therefore, of the utmost importance for what kind of presidency we have in America.

PUBLIC OPINION: ASCERTAINING THE SHAPE OF POPULAR EXPECTATIONS

The desirable shape of public opinion about political leadership is clearly stated in classical democratic theory. In general, public opinion should accord basic legitimacy, trust, and support to duly elected officials, so as to allow for effective leadership. But it should avoid being so uncritical as to induce arrogance in leaders, or so unrealistic as to bring about public cynicism when incumbents fail to measure up to false or unrealistic standards. Public attitudes on important specific issues need to be based on sufficient attentiveness, information, and reflection to allow for measured judgment. Lastly, and of great importance, both the general and specific components of public opinion need to be *relatively coherent,* so that political leaders, like a President, can understand them. Even under these favorable conditions, a democratic leader needs reliable means of ascertaining, with a certain amount of accuracy, the "voice of the people." The classical democratic theory of public opinion clearly asks much of citizens and leaders.

It is generally conceded that in recent years there has been a decline of general trust and support for the President from the general public. One indication of this may be that in the eighteen-year period from January 20, 1961 to January 20, 1979 each of the five different Presidents, at the same point in his first term, met with less public approval than his predecessor. Gallup documents this as follows.

Average Percent Who Approve in Months 25-30 of a President's First Term

	Percent
John F. Kennedy	66
Lyndon B. Johnson	54
Richard M. Nixon	50
Gerald R. Ford	47
Jimmy Carter	40

(Reported in Gallup Poll for WHYY, Inc., 1980)

The first of these was assassinated, the second forced not to seek reelection for a second term, the third compelled to resign, the fourth defeated in his bid for reelection, and the fifth experienced sharp swings in his popularity ratings throughout the entirety of his single term. Two basic difficulties have plagued the relationship of recent Presidents to public opinion. One has to do with the public's general expectations of the office. The other has to do with the difficulty in reading specific public attitudes on particular issues.

From Roosevelt's inauguration in 1933 to Nixon's resignation in 1974, the "climate of expectations" clearly supported a strong President. Americans came to look to the President for reassurance, a sense of progress and action, and for a sense of legitimacy. Thomas Cronin wrote near the end of the 1960s that Americans now look "toward their presidents to articulate national goals, unite the nation, explain the state of the nation— or the 'state of the world'—forecast the future and protect us from alien ideologies." (Cronin, 1970, pp. 34, 919) And Joe McGinnis, who as a young journalist worked in the Nixon campaign of 1968, quotes one memo circulated by the staff saying: "Potential candidates are measured against an ideal that's a combination of leading man, God, father, hero, pope-king with maybe just a touch of the avenging furies thrown in." (McGinnis, 1969, p. 26) Finally, Fred Greenstein described five psychological functions of the presidency which both enlarge the expectations of the office and magnify its status. The President (1) simplifies perception of government and politics; (2) provides an outlet for emotional expression; (3) is a symbol of unity; (4) provides people with a vicarious means of taking political action; and, (5) is a symbol of social stability. (Greenstein, 1966, p. 30)

This climate supporting a strong presidency reached its zenith in the 1960s and contributed directly to the arrogance of power that characterized the Johnson and Nixon administrations. As Richard Neustadt says, the public standing of a President, his prestige, gives him—more than anything else—"leeway." (Neustadt, 1980, p. 67) During the Johnson-Nixon years, the attitudes supporting a powerful presidency clearly gave incumbents too much leeway. The agonizing and, for Americans, unique loss in the Indochina War coupled with the sordid and highly publicized revelations about Watergate threw public expectations and perceptions about the presidency into a turmoil. It became unclear just what Americans generally expected of a President. Did they want a down-to-earth, hail-fellow-well-met and more-or-less ordinary "people's" President who offered little danger of consolidating and perhaps abusing power? Or, did they still yearn for a larger-than-life "monarchical" figure? Due to the confusion over this and the deep disenchantment occasioned by Johnson's and Nixon's actions, the requisite willingness of the citizenry to support presidential leadership (which is necessary— although not sufficient in itself—to make the fragmented political system work), may have been undermined.

President Carter clearly believed this was the case and, on June 15, 1979 made an extraordinary prime-time television address to the nation on this very theme. He began his speech by

asking: "Why have we not been able to get together as a nation
to resolve our serious energy problem?" The main reason, in
President Carter's view, was "a crisis or erosion of confidence."
He cited several examples of this, such as the fact that "two
thirds of our people do not even vote" and that "there is a
growing disrespect for government" as well as for other institutions. Among the causes he saw for this phenomenon are
some we have mentioned.

> We were sure that ours was a nation of the ballot, not
> the bullet, until the murders of John Kennedy and Robert
> Kennedy and Martin Luther King, Jr. We were taught that
> our armies were always invincible and our causes were
> always just, only to suffer the agony of Vietnam.

> We respected the presidency as a place of honor until the
> shock of Watergate.

The cynicism and disenchantment resulting from these events
were, to Carter, at least partly responsible for the fact that his
presidential tenure had not provided the kind of leadership
normally expected of incumbents. His detractors, on the other
hand, blamed him, and not the environment of political attitudes.

They pointed out that, as Carter's term neared its end,
memories of the Indochina War and the Watergate affair had
receded and people were looking for more effective presidential
leadership than he seemed able to provide. In a major poll taken
in late 1979, 63 percent said the United States needs strong
leadership. Only 49 percent had expressed this view in 1976.
Similarly, only 30 percent, versus 44 percent in 1976, saw such
strong leadership as dangerous. And only 8 percent believed the
President had too much power. This does not mean that the
population desired a return to the imperial presidency. When
asked which branch should have the major responsibility in
domestic policy areas, 37 percent said the President should,
36 percent said Congress, and 22 percent wanted equal responsibility. What the public sought was clearly revealed in their
response to the question concerning which qualities they desired
most in a President. The trait that showed the greatest increase
in public desirability from 1974 to 1979 was "political savvy,"
or the ability to provide effective political leadership. Thus, the
confused "climate of expectations" which characterized the mid-
to-late 1970s seems to have given way to a new but cautious
willingness to support strong, politically effective presidential
leadership. (Gallup Poll for WHYY, Inc., 1980)

A second problem in building effective linkages between the President and public opinion has to do with the questionable reliability of the devices which Presidents use to interpret the many cues the public gives them. Presidents face certain inherent difficulties in ascertaining the "will of the people" in our complex, diverse society, particularly on specific issues. Incumbents have used various means to try to accomplish this task. These include traveling about the country and meeting with people, perusing telegrams and letters, and scrutinizing selected media from throughout the nation. Presidents also seek to keep in touch with public attitudes by interacting with interest group leaders. Yet these devices only allow the President to glimpse a small part of the totality of American public opinion. Often, the impressions he gains from them are distorted.

Presidents have historically relied most of all on party channels of communication to keep them in touch with the wishes and feelings of the people. This began when Jefferson traveled about the small, young nation in the late 1790s building the Democratic-Republican Party on the basis of state and local "party clubs." It was clearly evident as late as Roosevelt's first term when the New Deal legislative programs were formulated largely in response to pressure from party ranks. The political party as a major device linking Presidents with the public has been undermined since WWII as the parties have become weaker and more disorganized.

A relatively new listening device, the public opinion poll, has emerged as the deficiencies of the older methods have become more apparent. Presidents have utilized polls for approximately the past twenty-five years. The first such use occurred, as political analyst Dom Bonafede notes, when Franklin Roosevelt retained Hadley Cantril of the Institute of Social Research in Princeton, N.J., to measure various attitudes of Americans before and during the United States' military involvement in World War II. All subsequent Presidents have relied to varying degrees on polls. Johnson was a devout aficionado of them, until they showed increasing dissatisfaction with his war policy. Presidents have periodically called upon a number of major polling organizations, among which are Market Opinion Research Corporation of Detroit, Opinion Research Corporation of Princeton, Public Research of Washington, as well as the better known Gallup and Louis Harris firms. Carter was the first "to have an in-house public opinion specialist who also functions as a political adviser and enjoys what amounts to White House staff status." This was Patrick Caddell. In the words of one of the most prominent men in the field, Peter Hart, no other pollster had ever been so "involved in the day-to-day operation of the White House." (Bonafede, 1978, pp. 1312-15)

How accurate and reliable are polls as a presidential guide to public opinion? Many people challenge polls' statistical reliability, but in fact they undoubtedly do indicate the sweep of public feelings in general and citizens' thinking on the particular issues which they examine. However, even this information leaves many attitudes untapped and a host of issues unexamined. One of the best, most concise critiques of polling, made some years back by Theodore J. Lowi, focused on these deficiencies. He asked in 1970, at the end of a tumultuous decade, what kind of political "system do we have that it can be impervious to social change and disorder?" Lowi's conclusion was that Establishment political leaders were generally unresponsive to the turmoil because they act on the questionable assumption that most Americans are political moderates who do not want changes in public policies, and they are reinforced in this belief by the false portrait of public attitudes presented by polls. This occurs for two major reasons.

> Polling agencies, first of all, ask only certain questions: there is simply no room for everything on the questionnaire. Often the only issues touched upon are those that have been on the agenda for some time, and it is probable that for many of these, opinion hovers around the center.

The neglect of latent, subterranean issues can cripple Presidents.

A second important factor in polling is the way in which questions are asked and responses are structured. On complex, ambiguous issues respondents will have "to pick a single response (either For or Against; or Strongly For, For, Against, Strongly Against—'Please check only one')." People are forced to cancel out a host of intense feelings and wishes. This makes for, in Lowi's assessment, a lot of meaningless, moderate "net responses." Consequently "the extremes are eliminated statistically." (Lowi, 1970, p. 205)

Polling data may be the scientific equivalent of those flickering and deceptive images cast on the cave walls by the fire in Plato's famous allegory. And Presidents who rely too heavily on polls to the exclusion of other devices as a guide to public opinion may be in a quandary similar to Plato's cave dwellers. They come to mistake illusion for reality. Since all the devices available to them are to some extent unreliable, incumbents must use a variety of "listening" devices, rather than rely too heavily on any one, even the "scientific" public opinion polls.

PRESIDENTIAL RESPONSIVENESS: PERSONALITY AND POLITICS

The second requirement for an effective public opinion process is that leaders must be compelled to heed and relate to it. This does not mean that Presidents should merely pander to public sentiment. Rather, they must find a path between this extreme and its opposite wherein the President imagines himself compromised each time he yields his own preferences to those of public opinion. Stipulating that a President must "heed and relate to" public opinion avoids both extremes. It allows the President to be more than simply an "instructed delegate" of the people while at the same time it does not allow him to act on his preferences alone as a "free agent."

There is a good deal of confusion in the United States over the degree to which Presidents are expected to be "free agents" or "instructed delegates." This makes it difficult to specify just how closely in tune with public attitudes presidential actions are expected to be. What appears to be the case is that on noncontroversial issues and/or those which do not intimately affect large numbers of people, such as bureaucratic reorganization, day-to-day foreign relations, and international trade matters, Presidents have a good deal of latitude. On highly salient issues, such as abortion, nuclear energy, civil rights, certain taxing and spending measures, and war policy, which attract strong feelings from either a large number of people, or from a vocal and strategically placed minority, Presidents must adhere more closely to the relevant public attitudes, or face the political consequences.

There are essentially two ways in which Presidents can be led to relate to public opinion. The first is through their own internal predispositions. According to Louis Koenig, the personal traits of the President are crucial when an ambitious, strong incumbent holds office at a time when the other branches are more inclined to support his power than to check it. In such times,

Koenig says, "The reconcilability of the strong President with the requisites of democracy depends crucially upon the personality of the incumbent, upon how well his values, character, and style harmonize with democratic ways." (Koenig, 1975; p. 327) He distinguishes between high and low democracy personality types. The former of these is personally secure but not arrogant, is open, accessible, and responsive, learns from criticism, and enjoys public interaction. The other is intolerant of criticism, feels insecure and acts aggressively to promote his own interest, is manipulative and secretive and tends to isolation, and is unresponsive to the suffering caused by festering problems. This type is by nature ill-suited to the needs of democratic leadership. We have, unfortunately, some recent examples.

The problems which ultimately caused Richard Nixon to lose political support and forced him from the White House were based in large part on some of the personality flaws Koenig identifies with the low-democracy model. This becomes clear as one peruses the Nixon transcripts of conversations dealing with the Watergate scandal. One finds the President ordering the payment of hush money, invoking national security claims to limit the investigation, implying that the Watergate burglars can expect clemency if they keep quiet about the involvement of administration figures, and directing that a list of political officials who fail to assist him be kept for future punishment. Although this is dismaying enough, there is something even more disheartening which finally proved his undoing. This is the total disregard for public concern about these actions. For example, in a meeting on March 21, 1973, President Nixon and White House Counsel John Dean exchanged the following words:

P. Frankly, all the people aren't going to care that much.
D. That's right.
P. People won't care, but people are going to be talking about it, there is no question.

It is also true that Johnson's inability to comprehend and heed the growing disenchantment with his Vietnam War policy after late 1965 was related to his personality. According to Doris Kearns, who came to know Johnson well, he tended to react to critics by maligning their motives, even on occasion imagining giant conspiracies against him. (Kearns, 1976; pp. 313-17)

Led by the pioneering work of James David Barber, political scientists in the 1970s devoted more careful attention to the link between presidential personality and democratic politics than they had done previously. However, as Barber and other scholars are well aware, there is no foolproof way to ensure that those reaching the White House will be "high-democracy" types who will heed the people's will. Thus, there is a need for political devices to compel Presidents to do so. This is the second major way in which Presidents are linked with public opinion.

There are a host of both indirect and direct means by which public opinion can be impressed upon a President. The direct ones include letters, phone calls, and telegrams to the President, protests, either peaceable ones protected under the First Amendment or violent ones, and the withdrawal of support from an incumbent seeking reelection. Indirect means include pressuring other political officials to pursue policies different from those of the President, expressing disapproval of the incumbent's specific policies or his overall handling of the office through responses to polls, and the withdrawal of electoral support from the President's political party. Two examples will illustrate how these direct and indirect methods can work to make a determined President heed public opinion.

In 1935 several major pieces of President Franklin Roosevelt's New Deal program were invalidated by the Supreme Court on various constitutional grounds. In 1936 he was reelected by the largest popular landslide in history. In 1937, shortly after his inauguration, Roosevelt convened cabinet and congressional leaders to brief them on a set of legislative proposals to reform the federal courts. The stated objective was to make the judiciary more efficient. The real object was political control of the Supreme Court. This was most clear in the proposal that the President would be allowed to appoint one new Supreme Court justice for every incumbent who failed to retire at seventy years of age.

The response from official circles, the media, and the public was quick and overwhelmingly negative. General public opposition was expressed in the largest outpouring of letters and telegrams to the President that had ever been received on any issue and in town meetings in New England and local meetings throughout the country which went on record as opposed. Leading farm organizations plus labor groups like the AFL and the CIO stated their opposition. Many constituents transmitted their sentiments to their political representatives in Congress. Roosevelt attempted to turn the tide of opinion. On March 4, 1937, he addressed thirteen-hundred Democratic party leaders in the Mayflower Hotel ballroom in Washington, D.C., instructing them to drum up support around the country. On March 9, 1937, Roosevelt spoke on a nationwide radio broadcast, appealing for public support. He failed. (Catledge, 1938)

Another dramatic example of a President's failure to anticipate public reaction was Richard Nixon's famous "Saturday Night Massacre" which occurred in October 1973 within a year of his overwhelming reelection victory over George McGovern. The "Saturday Night Massacre" developed as follows. As a condition of winning Senate confirmation of Attorney General Elliot Richardson, Nixon had agreed that Special Watergate Prosecutor Archibald Cox could follow investigative leads in the scandal wherever they might take him, with no interference from the President. On October 20, he reneged on this and ordered Richardson to fire Cox. Richardson refused and resigned. His deputy, William Ruckelshaus, likewise refused and was fired. Finally, Solicitor General Robert Bork did fire Cox. Nixon's press secretary, Ronald Ziegler, announced all this to a stunned nation.

Within hours of the announcement of Cox's firing, a massive wave of public protest descended on Washington. Thousands of people protested directly by sending letters, telegrams, and telephone calls to the White House and other parts of the government. The representatives of the people spoke out. Democrats in the House of Representatives drafted impeachment resolutions. The AFL-CIO called upon the President to resign. Republicans in Congress also began to desert the President.

Failure to anticipate the public reaction to Cox's firing was a serious, and perhaps fatal, error on the part of the Nixon administration. Nixon's standing in the polls plummeted immediately, and he never regained any of the public support which he lost. His days were numbered after this event.

A number of things are striking about the way the public opinion process worked in these two instances. In both cases it was generally negative in nature. It was aroused and had its impact only after the fact of an unpopular presidential action. It was brought into play only periodically. Because of these limits on the expression of public opinion, Presidents normally have a good deal of latitude in exercising leadership. However, they must always act on the basis of the "anticipated reaction" of the public. The periodic expression of an aroused public opinion through the direct and indirect channels available to it reinvigorates its vitality and sharpens the President's sensitivity to public reaction.

DEMOCRATIC PERSUASION: THE "BULLY PULPIT"

The third requirement of a public opinion process which links the President and the people is that the former must possess the proper tools for effective, nonauthoritarian public persuasion. When ex-President Nixon was asked in a recent interview what he considered to be the three or four most important abilities a President must have, he cited among these "the ability to persuade people individually and in the general public to support his views." Public persuasion in a democracy requires the skillful use of the many channels of communication available to the President in a nonauthoritarian way.

When he was President, Nixon became frustrated with attempts to persuade or educate the public in this manner. Instead, he attempted to gain authoritarian control over the channels of communication and the flow of information and images presented to the public. As Dorothy James explains, several existing agencies were used in an effort to control the press, and one new one was created within the White House. This was the Office of Telecommunications Policy. One of the major efforts of those in this office was to draft legislative proposals which would have made local television stations individually responsible for all network news material they broadcast. If their network news and their local news were not "balanced," then stations would risk losing their licenses. The proposals never passed. The intent was to reduce the local station's inclination to carry network news programs and commentary, which the administration viewed as biased. Working out of this office, onetime communications director Herbert Klein warned the press publicly that if they failed to investigate their own bias, the government would step in and do so. Also, presidential aides Charles Colson and Clay Whitehead were dispatched to meetings with media elites around the country to stress that the administration was committed to the creation of what it saw as a fair press, even if it took such drastic action as breaking up the networks into smaller entities. After one such session in New York, Colson reported gleefully, "we've got those bastards on the run." And, in fact, the networks did stop commentary on presidential speeches for a time. (James, 1974, pp. 74-80)

The Justice Department, headed by former campaign director John Mitchell, used a variety of intimidation tactics in this effort. Newspaper reporters were pressured by subpoenas to reveal confidential news sources or risk jail terms. Television networks were threatened with antitrust suits. In addition to actions taken by the Justice Department, the Federal Communications Commission (headed by a former Nixon political associate) called on several television stations for transcripts of their editorial comments on Nixon's speeches.

Such activity can have a "chilling" or even paralyzing effect on independent and dynamic communication of political views in a democratic society. On the other hand, the nonauthoritarian approach to public persuasion can have just the opposite impact. It can stimulate the discussion of issues by members of the political society.

The democratic approach to public persuasion is to use "the bully pulpit," as Theodore Roosevelt termed the presidency, as a podium from which to engage in educating the public about why certain policies and programs need to be pursued. This teaching is done by presidential communications and actions. The former are transmitted to the nation through such things as dispensing background material to reporters, leaking favorable information, issuing press releases, radio and television interviews, and televised press conferences, and speeches from Washington and other places around the country.

Theodore Roosevelt and Woodrow Wilson were the first Presidents to capitalize on the communications possibilities of the presidency by holding regular press conferences and providing room in the White House for the press to work. Franklin D. Roosevelt expanded these conferences to biweekly sessions, refined the use of radio with his very effective "fireside chats," and hired the first press secretary, Stephen Early. The next major development in the use of communications occurred in the Kennedy administration. John Kennedy greatly expanded the presidential effort at press and public relations, increased the number of staff aides assigned to these areas, and used the television medium more effectively than any President before or since. By the time of the Nixon administration the communications and public relations efforts of the executive branch in general and the White House in particular had become an enormous operation.

The Office of Management and Budget estimated that in the first Nixon administration there were 6,144 people engaged in public relations, at a cost of $161,000,000 a year. Approximately 61 people on the White House staff itself were engaged in public relations, including about 12 people under Herbert Klein, 14 working for Ronald Zeigler, and a third group directed by Charles Colson. (Edelman in Barber, 1974, pp. 169-70)

The significance of presidential communications continued to accelerate in the 1970s. One of Jimmy Carter's closest and most important advisers was his press secretary, Jody Powell. Surveying the growth and scope of presidential communications, Dorothy James concludes that Presidents have power "in defining the issues, controlling the nature of debate, and reaching the public in a direct, unmediated fashion that is unavailable to any other institution or group within American society." (James, 1974, p. 80)

Despite the vast resources available to the President, there are inescapable limits to his power to persuade through communications. Indeed, it is highly unlikely that even the most imaginative communications and public relations strategy will bolster public support very long for Presidents whose actions are a cause for public concern. Lyndon Johnson's famous "credibility gap" is a case in point of a futile effort to explain away a failing Indochina War policy. As Neustadt says, "merchandising is no match for history." And, "a President's instruction is affected by his own performance." (Neustadt, 1980; pp. 72-77) Even so, all recent Presidents have turned to public relations experts and image-makers when they have encountered a drop in public support. The Nixon administration had an "image committee" which met weekly to devise strategies to bolster his standing. Midway in Carter's first term, when his approval rating dropped to a nadir of 28 percent, he called his former director of campaign advertising, Gerald Rafshoon, from Atlanta to a post in the White House. Rafshoon was to try to present the President in a better light to the media and the public. In both these instances, there is little evidence that the efforts at "image-making" had any appreciable effect on the two Presidents' fortunes.

A President risks losing public support when his words and his public relations image are clearly inconsistent with his actions. Richard Nixon's Attorney General John Mitchell, apparently unaware of this possibility, counseled on one occasion that people should "look at what we do and not what we say." The irony of that would haunt him and the others convicted in the Watergate scandal as the nation indeed looked carefully at what they did.

When a President's actions are consistent with his words, in touch with public expectations, and display an effort to deal effectively with the problems and needs of the people, he stands a much better chance of protecting his public prestige. Neustadt cites FDR's words and actions during the Depression of the 1930s as an example of a President protecting his public prestige in this way.

When Roosevelt assumed office in March 1933, over fifteen million were unemployed, millions lived in "Hooverville's," or shanty towns, more than one million wandered aimlessly about the country, and local relief and charity arrangements plus the efforts of state governments had failed. Industrial production was down by 50 percent since the crash in 1929, as was income, and the agricultural sector lay in shambles. Over five thousand banks had collapsed. Despair and a sense of hopelessness characterized the mood of the country. On March 4 Roosevelt went on nationwide radio to assure Americans that "we have nothing to fear but fear itself." This effort at teaching was followed by action. Otherwise, as Neustadt points out, "the lesson of those words would have been bitter for the country and his phrase would be remembered now with mockery not cheers." (Neustadt, 1980; p. 76) On March 9 Roosevelt temporarily closed the banks and convened a special session of Congress which sat for one hundred days until June 16. He submitted a program for "relief, recovery, and reform" that passed in unprecedented fashion stabilizing the banking system, providing public-works jobs, and supporting agricultural and industrial activity, among other things. This is a classic case where the President's words were reasonably consistent with the emergency actions which followed as well as the public expectations the words aroused. It illustrates how a President's teaching can be enormously effective when these conditions are met.

CONCLUSION

We have attempted in this essay to analyze the manner in which the public opinion process links the President with the American people. This analysis was conducted within the context of democratic theory. As we understand that theory, it requires that leaders must be able to ascertain the public will, feel compelled to heed or relate to this, and have available nonauthoritarian means for "public persuasion." In this fashion, what Madison called the "primary check," the people, can interact effectively with their leaders. Incumbents, in turn, have the opportunity to exercise proper leadership in the political society. This public opinion process may offer the best hope for preventing the resurgence of an "imperial" presidency, while avoiding the problems of an "imperiled" presidency. In looking at the relationship of recent Presidents and the public in these three areas, we found the following.

The public will is not always easy for Presidents to ascertain. This has been particularly true since "Johnson's War" (as the Indochina War was often termed) and the Watergate scandal threw public expectations into a turmoil. It is only recently, as memories of these things recede, that polls are beginning to show a more consistent, if cautious, willingness to support renewed presidential leadership. Another real problem in reading public wishes lies in the demise of traditional devices, like political parties, which were useful for this purpose. There is an increasing reliance on public opinion polls. While they are certainly helpful, they may ignore key issues and overly simplify—and hence distort—public attitudes on other ones. Presidents need a variety of devices.

In turning to the question of how Presidents can be led to heed or relate to—which is not the same thing as pandering to—public opinion, we find two major ways this occurs. One is through their personal inclinations to heed the public. What Koenig calls "high-democracy" types are inclined to do this, while "low-democracy" types are inclined to isolation and the avoidance of public interaction. Political actions such as protests, letters, and telegrams, and the withdrawal of electoral support are external ways in which incumbents can be compelled to heed the public. When Presidents severely violate the limits of public tolerance by their actions, these can be decisive in controlling or punishing them. This makes it more likely that their successors will govern with the "anticipated reaction" of the public in mind.

Lastly, we found that effective public persuasion is the very essence of leadership in a democratic society. American Presidents have ample access to the communications channels necessary for this. For a host of reasons some Presidents may seek to control public debate by intimidating and manipulating the media. This endangers rather than serves a democratic society. The most effective Presidents, those who make the greatest contribution to American society and find the most ready acceptance, are those whose rhetoric is reasonably consistent with their actions, is in touch with public expectations, and addresses important issues.

Suggested Readings

Bonafede, Dom. "Carter and the Polls—If You Live by Them, You May Die by Them." *National Journal* (August 19, 1978): 1312-15.

Catledge, Turner and Alsop, Joseph W. *168 Days.* Garden City, N.Y.: Doubleday Doran and Co., 1938.

Cronin, Thomas E. "The Textbook Presidency and Political Science." *Congressional Record* (October 5, 1970): 34920+.

Edelman, Murray. "The Politics of Mass Persuasion." *Choosing the President,* pp. 149-73. Edited by James D. Barber. Englewood Cliffs, N.J.: Prentice Hall, Inc., 1974.

Gallup Poll. "Attitudes Toward the Presidency." The Gallup Organization (January 1980).

Greenstein, Fred I. "The Psychological Functions of the Presidency for Citizens." *The American Presidency: Vital Center,* pp. 29-36. Edited by Elmer E. Cornell. Chicago: Scott, Foresman, 1966.

James, Dorothy Buckton. *The Contemporary Presidency.* 2d ed. New York: The Bobbs-Merrill Company, Inc., 1974.

Kearns, Doris. *Lyndon Johnson and the American Dream.* New York: Harper & Row, 1976.

Koenig, Louis W. *The Chief Executive.* New York: Harcourt, Brace, Jovanovich, Inc., 1975.

Lowi, Theodore J. "The Artificial Majority." *The Nation* 211, No. 19 (December 7, 1970): 591-94.

McGinnis, Joseph. *The Selling of the President, 1968.* New York: Trident Press, 1969.

Neustadt, Richard E. *Presidential Power.* 2d ed. New York: John Wiley & Sons, Inc., 1980.

2

The President and the News Media

Robert Locander
North Harris County College, Houston

American Presidents are not required constitutionally to meet the press; the news media have no formal obligation to cover the Chief Executive, but the two have entered into a common-law relationship in which each partner receives substantial rewards from this marriage.

All modern Presidents from Franklin Roosevelt to Jimmy Carter have wanted to communicate with the public, and the mass media have proven to be an effective channel for fulfilling this desire. At a fundamental level, the relationship between the President and the news media can be understood as a series of interactions involving the exchanges of executive information for media publicity.

It is important to understand the gravitating pull of power which draws the President and the news media together. Since FDR's time, the executive's power in the American political system has grown so great that critics talked of an imperial presidency. During the decade of the 1960s, the news media's power became a recognized political force in the country. In a 1974 *U.S. News & World Report* national survey, a sample population rated television as the most powerful American institution, even out-polling the White House which finished second. (USNWR, 4/22/74, pp. 30-35)

WHY PRESIDENTS COMMUNICATE
THROUGH THE NEWS MEDIA

While a general explanation for presidential communication might be that power seeks power, there are four specific reasons behind a President's decision to communicate. The first reason is simply that presidential communication has come to be expected. If newsmen cannot question the President regularly at press conferences, columnists and editorial writers will begin sniping at the closed White House.

Along with media representatives, the public has its own expectations of Presidents and wants to know what the person symbolizing the nation has to say about serious and light subjects. Other groups expecting presidential messages are congressmen, bureaucrats, lobbyists, foreign government officials, and state and local candidates. These individuals want a President to speak out so they might receive legislative backing, program support, substantive and symbolic benefits, policy reassurances, and election boosts from the man in the White House.

A second reason for presidential communication is that an executive desires to sell his administration's programs to the country and the Congress. Through a press conference, personal interview, national television address, or fireside chat, the President may try to mobilize opinions and votes to his side. Before he had been in office a week, Roosevelt delivered the first of his famous radio fireside chats in 1933 to a depression-troubled nation. A soothing and confident voice went out to a people beset with economic worries and assured them of the new administration's intention to straighten out America's banking and fiscal ills. After the address, Will Rogers quipped that F.D.R. had taken a complicated subject like banking and made everybody understand it, even the bankers.

The concern over reelection is a third reason why first-term executives communicate with the press and the public. Presidents are politically ambitious men and their desire to remain in office is strong. Even atypical modern executives like Dwight Eisenhower, a professional soldier, and Gerald Ford, an accidental President with a congressional outlook, decided to run for the White House when they could have retired gracefully into private life.

While the official campaign begins in the early part of a presidential year with the New Hampshire primary, challengers and an eligible incumbent have been campaigning unofficially for years. Like the lengthened sports season featuring football in July and baseball in October, the presidential race has changed from a sprint into a marathon. Throughout his first term, a President will be traveling and speaking to many audiences. His messages will be explanations of administration policies, expressions of good will, calls for national support, and advertisements for himself.

The charge of running for the White House from inside the Oval Office is raised frequently against the Presidents. Despite efforts at campaign reform, it is unlikely that the great political advantages the office of the presidency offers its occupant can ever be legislated away. In the words of Theodore Roosevelt, Presidents possess a "bully pulpit" and deliver subtle reelection sermons for years prior to any balloting.

As has been shown, Presidents communicate because they are expected to, they want to sell their policy programs, and they desire reelection. The final reason for presidential communication is that it serves the personal needs of the Chief Executive. Presidents find it rewarding to address enthusiastic crowds and receive the psychic lift that a cheering audience can provide.

Despite the dangers of assassination, executives have continued to travel openly and plunge into crowds. Following a close brush with death, President Ford insisted that he would not become a prisoner of the White House. Ford's attitude may have had the public in mind, but presidential trips outside Washington are still ego-satisfying and therapeutic experiences. The complexities of issues and pressures of the position are washed away for a time as a President bathes in the warm and comforting embrace of an adoring audience.

In addition to receiving immediate psychological rewards, Presidents communicate out of a concern for their place in history. Some executives even created the informal post of historian in residence to ensure that the "true" story of their administrations might be told. John Kennedy selected Arthur Schlesinger, Jr., to fill this role, while Eric F. Goldman served Lyndon Johnson in this capacity. One of the reasons for Richard Nixon's secret tape recording of White House conversations was a concern about future accounts of his administration. It was Nixon's claim that President Johnson gave him this idea based on his own tape-recording for "history's" sake.

PRESIDENTIAL COMMUNICATIONS STYLES

After offering four reasons for presidential communication, our next concern will be to examine the different styles exhibited by modern Presidents in their media relations. A President's communications style consists of the attitudes and behavior he exhibits in his relationship with news people. The communications style of an executive is important because it affects his overall press relations. Recent history has shown that the news media contributed to the collapse of the Johnson and Nixon presidencies, while the Roosevelt and Kennedy presidencies were aided immeasurably by their media genius and playful relationship with reporters.

What different communications styles have modern Presidents exhibited in their press relations? Modern Presidents can be classified according to three style-types: "masters and friends," "naive and unaffected," and "paranoid and unforgiving."

Franklin Roosevelt and John Kennedy are representatives of the "masters and friends" communications style. This type of President demonstrates great skills as a publicist. He is able to communicate effectively using the mass media as an important tool of presidential leadership. The master and friend is relaxed around reporters and understands the needs of journalists. His administration makes an effort to cooperate fully with the press's demands for information. The President expects to receive criticism and handles complaints affably by acting upon the legitimate grievances and turning aside other accusations without rancor.

In their media relations, Roosevelt and Kennedy displayed great skills. As communicators, their talents were unmatched by any other Presidents in this century with the possible exception of Theodore Roosevelt. Both FDR and JFK were media pioneers using radio and television to their full political advantage. These two Democratic executives possessed such personal attributes as a charismatic personality, a dramatic speaking voice, a quick wit, a likable manner, and an understanding of the journalistic profession, all of which are traits spelling media success.

The "naive and unaffected" presidential communications style has been displayed by Harry Truman, Dwight Eisenhower, Gerald Ford, and Jimmy Carter. Often an inexperienced or uneasy media performer, a naive and unaffected President shows a certain uneasiness with words and ideas which causes him difficulty with a national press that admires urbane executives. Although an administration headed by this type of President does not battle the press like the paranoid and unforgiving executive, he refuses to accommodate newspeople like the masters and friends. The reaction of naive and unaffected Presidents to press criticism is to dismiss complaints, both the valid and the petty. These presidents aim to please the public and themselves but not necessarily news people.

As media performers, Truman, Eisenhower, Ford, and to a lesser extent Carter were amateurs compared to Roosevelt and Kennedy. These four Presidents had their problems in answering the national press's questions. Truman and Carter possessed a penchant for quick, careless replies to serious queries which their press secretaries often had to clarify afterward, while Eisenhower and Ford bored reporters with homilies when a short, direct answer was the appropriate reply.

Although their press attitudes varied, not one of the four had what might be considered a healthy media outlook. To Truman and Eisenhower, the press was something one had to put up with during their presidencies. In the case of Eisenhower, James Hagerty, his press secretary, had to convince him to be tolerant as he talked the former general out of his plan to forego any presidential press conferences. Ford and Carter showed their unhappiness with the Washington press corps by using their own communications techniques, such as national television addresses, local press briefings, townhall meetings, and people press conferences, as ways of bypassing the national media.

Lyndon Johnson and Richard Nixon are examples of Presidents whose communications style was referred to earlier as "paranoid and unforgiving." In their interactions with the press, Presidents in this category experience major difficulties. They want total control of their messages and feel betrayed when the media display any independence. These executives blame the national press for their administration's problems.

Unable to understand or accept the press's critical function, the paranoid and unforgiving President is quick to feel that the media are conspiring against him for political or ideological reasons. While naive and unaffected executives generally are oblivious to what the press is saying about them, the paranoid and unforgiving, like the masters and the friends, are egoists.

They lack the skills, personality, and drama, however, to receive the press notices they seek. What the relationship between these men and the press evolves into is an us-and-them, friends-and-enemies relationship.

No other executives in the twentieth century had the press problems of Johnson and Nixon. Their relationships with the news media were marked by suspicion, contempt, and hatred. Why did these two Presidents fail so miserably in dealing with news people? Aside from similar personalities that could not accept critical comments, Johnson and Nixon lived a fantasy existence at the White House. After leaving the White House, George Reedy, a Johnson press secretary, wrote an influential book about presidential isolation from the real world outside the executive palace. (Reedy, 1970) If Reedy's thesis is correct, then the press served as the only messenger of gloom to the royal courts of Johnson and Nixon. This factor alone may explain why these two Presidents, protected and praised by sycophants, recoiled from the press's realistic revelations.

PRESIDENTIAL MESSENGERS TO THE NEWS MEDIA

In his relationship with the news media, a President needs help and receives it from two major assistants—his press secretary and his director of communications. As a presidential spokesman, the press secretary will meet with national reporters on a daily basis to brief them on the executive's schedule, issue policy statements, listen to any complaints or recommendations, and field questions on all kinds of matters.

The post of press secretary officially dates back to 1929, although Joseph Tumulty, an aide to Woodrow Wilson, can be considered the first person to perform the duties associated with this job on a full-time basis. From Tumulty's time to the present, press secretaries have been faced with the dilemma of serving as the President's spokesman and acting as the news media's intermediary to the White House. The potential for role conflict in this position is great, and some press secretaries have found themselves discredited because they overacted as the President's man.

On the importance of a press secretary for an executive's media relations, Merriman Smith, a former UPI White House correspondent, has written, "The job of press secretary is well known to the public, but its importance is hard to overrate. A press secretary can make or break a modern White House administration, because a President's chief strength lies in his ability to get his ideas, programs, and principles across to the public." (Smith ed., 1972, pp. 95-96)

The examples of James Hagerty and Ronald Ziegler illustrate Smith's point about the importance of press secretaries. During the Eisenhower's years, Hagerty displayed a genius for public relations. He served well the press secretary's three constituencies—the President, the news media, and the public. No question existed over Hagerty's performance in serving Eisenhower's interests, but he also carried out well his responsibilities to the press and the public. It is generally recognized that James Hagerty was the most technically proficient modern press secretary. He was a master at turning out letter-perfect news releases and ensuring that reporters were provided with copies of presidential messages well in advance of their deadlines.

Reporters respected Hagerty for two reasons. First, he showed a genuine concern for reporters and looked out for their interests. Eisenhower's press secretary made certain that the President's travel plans were arranged with the press in mind. Second, he was direct, honest, and knowledgeable in talking with reporters. Throughout his association with Eisenhower, Hagerty's press credibility remained high which was not the case with several of his successors.

Ron Ziegler, Nixon's press secretary, was not only inexperienced in the folkways of Washington journalism, but was neither technically proficient in his job nor a believable news source. Despite these three strikes against him, Ziegler held on to his position, a sure sign of one President's contemptuous feelings toward the press. Even prior to his false statements about Watergate, some reporters questioned his truthfulness and credibility. In 1971, James Naughton of *The New York Times* reported that some journalists were convinced that "Ziegler is hardly more than a Pinocchio puppet whose nose does not grow when he fibs." (Wise, 1973, p. 278)

Another of Ziegler's problems as press secretary was his evasiveness in answering reporters' questions. A vague and imprecise speaker, he was presented with a "gobbledy-gook" award by a teachers group interested in preserving clear speech. In response to a question about the Watergate tapes, which could have been answered with a "yes," a "no," or an "I don't know," Ziegler's award-winning response was a 99-word, incomplete sentence. While the press secretary is the President's messenger to national newsmen, the director of communications is the White House's liaison with the local press. This position officially was created during the Nixon presidency. In 1969, Herbert Klein became the first director of the Office of Communications. During the Watergate investigations, critics of the office and Klein's successor, Kenneth Clawson, claimed that it was too much of a propaganda machine for a democratic government to harbor. Despite this criticism, President Ford decided to keep this agency going during his administration, and Jimmy Carter did likewise, although it was renamed the Office of Media Liaison in 1977.

The director and the Office of Communications attempt to ensure that the executive's viewpoints are carried outside Washington and the exclusive coverage of the national news media. This has been accomplished through letter-writing campaigns, direct mail projects, and regional briefings. The Nixon, Ford, and Carter administrations have all worked at achieving grass-roots support for their policies, but the Nixon White House got caught when it moved from mobilizing public opinion to manufacturing it.

According to the *United Press International* news service, a taped speech of Vice-President Spiro Agnew was scheduled for broadcast one weekend in December of 1969 over a number of the nation's radio stations, but Agnew's speech was not aired due to technical problems. Despite this fact, the UPI office in New York was flooded with 14,000 letters the following week praising the Vice-President's latest attack on liberals (Parenti, 1974, p. 177)

Besides encouraging letter-writing campaigns from supporters, the Office of Communication mailed news releases, government reports, and position papers to the local press in the hope of receiving favorable coverage. In August of 1976, President Ford continued a tradition begun by his predecessor of having a book chronicling his achievements in office sent to newspapers and stations throughout the country. This book highlighting the first two years of the Ford administration contained no criticism of the President.

The regional briefing is the third tactic coordinated by communications directors to get around a critical news media and present a President and his message to the local press and their audiences. In the first year of his presidency, President Carter held twenty-one press conferences with national newsmen and nineteen question-and-answer sessions with local editors and news directors. The format of these sessions was to have thirty to forty out-of-town media representatives come to the White House about every two weeks for briefings with officials and a short meeting with the President. Commenting on the value of this format for the participants at the January 26, 1979 briefing, Carter said, "It's helped us to understand the attitude and concern around the nation. And I hope it's been helpful in letting the people of different communities understand how our White House operated and what the key issues were at a particular moment." (*Weekly CPD*, 2/5/79, p. 9)

PRESIDENTIAL-MEDIA PATTERNS

To understand the relationship between modern Presidents and the news media, it is helpful to recognize that three continuing patterns can be found throughout the press's coverage of Presidents from Roosevelt to Carter: "abnormal cooperation," "the adversary relationship," and "abnormal conflict."

Abnormal cooperation between the White House and the news media occurs at times when reporters are extremely reverent and submissive in covering the executive. There is an absence of press criticism of the President and an unusual willingness to accept the White House's version of events. Specific periods of abnormal presidential-press cooperation occur during the honeymoon period for new Presidents, during a foreign-policy crisis, and at the death of an executive in office.

When a new administration takes office in Washington, the news media, like the Congress and public, traditionally extend the President and his assistants a period in which the spirit of cooperation and tolerance for mistakes are high. Depending on the President and events, this honeymoon period can last anywhere from a few months to a year and a half. In Harry Truman's case, there generally was shock and disbelief among news people when he took office upon Roosevelt's death. Despite their doubts, fears, and questions about his qualifications, reporters responded to Truman's pleas for their prayers and help at his first press conference by emphasizing his positive traits and overlooking his shortcomings in their stories during the interregnum.

The honeymoon period is not the only time when the news media display abnormal cooperation with the White House. Presidents also receive media assistance during a foreign policy crisis. The kinds of press cooperation include killing stories, slanting articles, and reporting events without challenging the government's account. The Vietnam War represented a situation in which the news media readily accepted Washington policies for years without challenging any of the official assumptions related to the war.

Vietnam did mark a break from World War II and the Korean War, however, because a few young correspondents, David Halberstam, Neil Sheehan, and Charles Mohr, refused to become a member of the Pentagon's team by reporting only the Defense Department's picture of the war. As a correspondent for *Time* magazine, Mohr's experience is revealing in that his Vietnam dispatches were rewritten in the weekly's Washington headquarters to reflect the official war story. (Rivers, 1967 pp. 120-21)

Along with the honeymoon period and the foreign-policy crisis, the press intentionally is uncritical following a President's death in office. The death of a President, whether he is a Franklin Roosevelt or a Warren G. Harding, will result in a sympathetic outpouring from the press hailing the passing of a martyr from America's midst. The temporary greatness of all Presidents is assured should they die in office.

The adversary relationship often is the general characterization used to describe modern presidential-press relations. It is unfortunate that the term "adversaries" has been used throughout the years to refer to news people and officials. The problem with this description is that it brings up images of heated courtroom struggles between two lawyers shouting back and forth at each other. In his book on the press and the government, George Berdes has come closest to describing the normal, day-to-day situation between a President and the news media by entitling his work, *The Friendly Adversaries.*

In facing an adversary press, modern Presidents encounter news people who will ask them questions about their actions, check out campaign promises, put current events into an historical context, and offer a different set of priorities for the nation's political agenda. All of these activities fall within the basic function of the American press which is informing the people of newsworthy events. As a government adversary, the news media's reporting sometimes benefits the President or on occasion causes him political harm, but most often press accounts of the White House have a neutral effect.

The presidential press conference today is the main public forum in which the adversary relationship between the executive and news people can be witnessed by millions of people on television. This situation has not always been the case, however, because in Roosevelt's time the conference was a private dialogue between the President and a handful of reporters crowded around his desk without any cameras or microphones. Since 1961, the meeting between adversaries has become a television news special attended by 350-to-400 journalists and broadcast to the nation.

As a communications channel, the press conference makes certain demands on any President. To be successful, an executive must be a quick thinker, adroit speaker, clever wit, good sport, and an information bank. Presidents Roosevelt, Kennedy, and Carter met these requirements and reaped great benefits in terms of press respect and public support, while for Truman, Eisenhower, Johnson, Nixon, and Ford, the press conference was a checkered experience. During the modern presidential period, Franklin Roosevelt holds the record for the most conferences —998—over twelve years in office, while in a little less than half that time Richard Nixon faced the press only 38 times.

Through his refusal to see reporters regularly, Nixon bore the ire of journalists who felt deprived of their right to meet the President. It may have been an attempt to avoid this type of situation which caused President Carter at his first press conference on February 8, 1977, to announce his intention to hold twice-a-month meetings with the press during his presidency. Carter made good on his promise during the first year in the White House, but by 1979, the President abandoned regular conferences preferring to meet with news people on an unscheduled basis.

While the adversary relationship is the most widely recognized presidential-media pattern, unusual conflict like unusual cooperation can be found throughout the period of the modern presidency. To an unprecedented degree in American history, the Nixon administration waged a war with the news media in 1969-70 over the question of fairness and objectivity. The purpose behind this war on "Agnewism" was to undermine the public's confidence in the three television networks and to frighten media representatives away from criticizing the administration. The Nixon-Agnew charges of a liberal media conspiracy bent on destroying the White House and subsequent legal and political campaigns against the press far outweighed what other administrations had done to deter news "slanted" against them. In Nixon's war with the news media, it is difficult to determine a winner; the White House appeared to win the opening battle as one research study revealed that television reporters cut back on the amount of personal interpretation of news events following Vice-President Agnew's two major speeches attacking the television networks. (Lowry, 1971, pp. 205-14) The tenacity displayed by reporters in covering the Watergate story, however, cannot be attributed solely to their desire for the truth. Some news people were no doubt motivated to repay Nixon for wounds suffered in previous battles.

Abnormal conflict between a President and the news media also happened during the Johnson years. LBJ's major struggles with the media stemmed from the presence of a "credibility gap." The press used this term to represent the disparity between actual events and the administration's description of those events. In the middle 1960s, Douglas Kiker of *The New York Herald Tribune* said of President Johnson that he "grandly mixes truth, half-truth, and non-truth and dares you to attempt to isolate them." (Quoted in Roberts, 1965, p. 118)

Johnson's personality certainly was responsible for some of his press problems. His hyperbolic manner of speaking and exaggerated versions of events often were at variance with reality. Reporters became cynical and doubted the President's Vietnam statements as the war became the focal point of his administration. The news media began opposing LBJ as huge gaps were uncovered between the administration's war accounts and what reporters and foreign observers witnessed in Vietnam.

As public dissent grew into an antiwar movement, Johnson blamed the press for his unpopularity and troubles. Correspondents were branded as "crybabies," "bellyachers," and Kennedy supporters who would not give him a fair shake. When Lyndon Johnson decided against running for a second full presidential term, his credibility with the press and the public was eroded completely. Like Nixon after him, Johnson's downfall can be attributed partly to the news media's revelations of facts that challenged the White House's versions of events.

ENDURING ISSUES

Historic events—Kennedy and the Missile Crisis, Johnson and Vietnam, Nixon and the China Trip, Ford and the Pardon, and Carter and Camp David, have affected, and sometimes changed, the relationship of a President and the news media. Without losing sight of any major event's power to influence the attitudes and behavior of Presidents and news people toward one another, several enduring presidential-press issues have affected and will continue to color this two-sided relationship.

The two enduring issues which stand out during the era of modern presidential-media relations are questions involving accuracy and access. The press is willing to accept a certain amount of White House shaping of events for political purposes, but reporters draw the line when presidential lying is uncovered. At these times, the news media will strike out hard against an administration in news stories and editorials.

The White House's defense of presidential lying is that the national interest must be protected at all costs and even truth must be sacrificed during an emergency period. As citizens themselves, reporters are not completely insensitive to this argument, but most would prefer a news blackout to executive lies. This choice is determined on the basis that truth is one of journalism's sacred precepts.

The American press and people were exposed to presidential lying in the 1950s when Eisenhower, a father figure representing honesty and sincerity to millions, was caught lying by the Soviets during the Francis Gary Powers incident. After the President denied any knowledge of United States aerial spy missions over Russia, Soviet Premier Nikita Khrushchev produced Powers, a U-2 pilot American intelligence experts assumed to be dead.

Following the Johnson and Nixon presidencies in which truth was a stranger, Jimmy Carter made personal honesty and integrity a major campaign theme in 1976. His famous promise about never lying to the American people was a reassuring message to the public, even if the press corps became increasingly skeptical of the claim.

On the accuracy issue, the press is concerned about presidential truth, while what the White House is looking for is fair and balanced reporting. Like examples of presidential lying, charges of media bias are common from the time of Roosevelt to Carter. All Presidents have criticized the press over its coverage of the White House. Franklin Roosevelt was bitter over what he perceived to be an anti-New Deal or Tory press that propagandized against his policies in the nation's newspapers. His successor, Harry Truman, often grumbled about the blatant Republican bias of the press throughout his White House years. Richard Nixon authorized a vicious attack against the biases of an Eastern, liberal press. As President-elect, Jimmy Carter complained about the television news coverage of his campaign and suggested that it nearly cost him the election.

Like accuracy, the access question is an enduring issue between modern Presidents and the press. As the accuracy issue has its extreme points of presidential lying and media bias, the ends of the access issue present the President as media superstar on one side and withdrawn mystery man on the other. Regardless of who is President, the press designates the executive as America's number one newsmaker. The coverage of the person in the White House is phenomenal, and news requests are endless for interviews and information about personal matters and affairs of state. It may be a surprise to some that a problem of overexposure has arisen during several administrations.

Political opponents and even some members of the news media have faulted Presidents for trying to dominate the nation's television screens through the use of prime-time speeches. These speeches allowed executives an opportunity for video domination in advancing their political ideas and policies. Until the Ford presidency, not one executive branch request for television time had been denied.

Richard Nixon's use of prime-time television was the most extensive among modern Presidents as he often substituted a network address in place of a press conference where he felt national reporters were out to "nail the chief" by asking impertinent or embarrassing questions. During the first eighteen months of his presidency, Nixon appeared on prime-time television as many times as the combined appearances of Presidents Eisenhower, Kennedy, and Johnson for a similar period.

Jimmy Carter showed an unprecedented television flurry early in his presidency with three televised appearances in a single week. What prompted Carter to become a mini-series was the energy issue, the President's moral equivalent of war. From April 18 to April 22, 1979, Carter addressed the nation on television, presented a televised speech to the Congress, and held a television press conference with reporters. Many of his political critics charged that "Carter, Energy, and Television" should not be allowed to go into reruns. Only time will tell if a future President attempts to exploit the networks for three days of broadcasting in the same week.

From the news media's perspective, the access issue strikes hardest when a President withdraws from the press's spotlight and assumes the role of a mystery man. The strongest complaints about the executive as superstar dominating the airways have come from congressmen, political opponents, and reformers. Their argument centers on demands for equal time to present another viewpoint. Although sympathetic to this demand, most news people are more troubled by presidential withdrawal from media exposure.

When reporters feel cut off from the President and key administration figures, news stories will appear about a "closed" White House. Since the Nixon presidency, which many reporters likened to covering the Kremlin, Gerald Ford and Jimmy Carter started their administrations with strong pledges to the press of openness and cooperation. The open state lasted throughout their honeymoon periods when the Nixon pardon and the Lance affair brought Ford and Carter respectively into a period of withdrawal from the news media.

To a large extent, White House correspondents have always been prisoners of their beat. This circumstance became most apparent when the Watergate story was missed by the White House press corps. With so many advantages on their side, it is surprising that Presidents should ever be accused of hiding in the Oval Office and dodging the press, but this occurs during most administrations.

Aside from the desire to avoid questioning during periods of political setback and scandal, many executives act as mystery men around reporters because of the time involved in preparing for a media encounter. Few Presidents will face reporters unless they have been well briefed and rehearsed, although many will not go to the lengths of former Secretary of State Dean Rusk. In his press meetings, Secretary Rusk carried a book along with him containing information separated into three subject headings; likely questions to be asked, recommended answers, and the true facts pertinent to the subject. (*Newsweek*, 4/18/63, pp. 59-63)

CONCLUSION

The presidency and the news media are powerful institutions and will continue as prominent features in the American political system of the 1980s. This article has focused on some of the modern keys to understanding the whys and hows of the relationship between Presidents and news people. The unchanging factors in this relationship are the reasons for presidential communication, the presidential-media patterns, and the enduring issues. The difficulty in predicting just what the future of presidential-media relations will be resides in the human factor because the type of person in the White House affects the presidential communications style and the kinds of messengers employed to the news media and their roles. It is interesting to speculate how John Kennedy's relationship with the press might have been had he lived and the United States policy in Vietnam been the same or how differently Washington correspondents would have treated Richard Nixon if his press secretary had been James Hagerty instead of Ronald Ziegler.

Suggested Readings

*Bagdikian, Ben H. *The Effete Conspiracy*, New York: Harper Colophon Books, 1974.

Berdes, George R. *The Friendly Adversaries: The Press and Government.* (Marquette University: The Center for the Study of the American Press, 1969.)

*Cater, Douglass, *The Fourth Branch of Government.* Boston: Houghton Mifflin, 1959.

Cornwell, Elmer E. Jr. *Presidential Leadership of Public Opinion.* Bloomington: Indiana University Press, 1965.

*Epstein, Edward J. *News From Nowhere.* New York: Vintage Books, 1973.

*Gans, Herbert J. *Deciding What's News.* New York: Pantheon Books, 1979.

*Halberstam, David. *The Powers That Be.* New York: Alfred A. Knopf, 1979.

*Johnston, David H. *Journalism and the Media.* New York: Barnes & Noble Books, 1979.

Minow, Newton N,; Martin, John Bartlow; and Mitchell, Lee M. *Presidential Television.* New York: Basic Books, 1973.

*Nessen, Ron. *It Sure Looks Different From the Inside.* New York: Playboy Press, 1979.
*Pollard, James E. *The Presidents and the Press: Truman to Johnson.* Washington, D.C.: Public Affairs Press, 1964.
*Porter, William E. *Assault on the Media.* Ann Arbor: The University of Michigan Press, 1976.
*Purvis, Hoyt. *The Presidency and the Press.* Austin: The University of Texas Press, 1976.
Small, William J. *Political Power and the Press.* New York: W.W. Norton & Company, 1972.
*Spragens, William C. *The Presidency and the Mass Media in the Age of Television.* Washington, D.C.: University Press of America, 1979.
*Wicker, Tom. *On Press.* New York: Berkley Book, 1979.

Other References Cited

*Dennis T. Lowry, "Agnew and the Network TV News: A Before/After Content Analysis," *Journalism Quarterly* 48 (Summer 1971), pp. 205-214.

Michael Parenti, *Democracy for the Few,* 1st ed. (New York: St. Martin's Press, 1974), p. 177.

George Reedy, *The Twilight of the Presidency* (New York: World Publishing, 1970).

This incident is related in William L. Rivers, *The Opinion Makers* (Boston: Beacon Press, 1967), pp. 120-121.

Kiker's quotation is from Charles Roberts, *LBJ's Inner Circle* (New York: Pelacorte Press, 1965), p. 118.

Timothy G. Smith, ed., *Merriman Smith's Book of Presidents* (New York: W. W. Norton & Co., 1972), pp. 95-96.

David Wise, *The Politics of Lying* (New York: Vintage Books, 1973), p. 278.

Weekly Compilation of Presidential Documents (Volume 15-Number 5), February 5, 1979, p. 9.

---

*Available in paperback.

Jimmy Carter visits people at home. *(Karl Schumacher, The White House)*

3

The President and Interest Groups

Joseph Pika
SUNY at Buffalo

Americans have traditionally emphasized ways in which the presidency unifies our decentralized and disparate political and social system. As chief of state, symbol of the nation, leader in foreign affairs and the only officeholder chosen from a national constituency, Presidents occupy a position which allows them to address needs, goals, and purposes of all the people. And, it is undeniably true that Presidents sometimes at least appear to behave in this way when they justify action on the basis of national interest even if there may be some doubt about the "real" reasons for their behavior.

Despite this image of uniquely *national* leadership, we have a President of parts as well as the whole. This inherent feature of the office has often been traced to "political" aspects of the job which are found in a President's need to form "electoral" and "governing" coalitions. The process followed in selecting Presidents requires that support be collected from various portions of the public at two stages. First, elements within the party organization must be united in order to win the nomination; then, appeals for support are made to a wider array of social groups as part of the general election strategy. Thus, presidential candidates need to form two electoral coalitions.

Once in office, Presidents need to form a "governing" coalition which may differ substantially from the backing which helped them get elected. This process, perhaps best described by

Richard Neustadt in *Presidential Power,* finds Presidents seeking support from groups in the Washington community (Congress, bureaucrats, and national media) as well as from distinct "publics" outside the capital. Presidents sustain their electoral and governing coalitions by exchanging favors and assistance with groups and influential individuals.

In particular, interest-group leaders seek to enlist the President as an ally in pursuing their policy goals and therefore initiate bargaining contacts with the executive, themselves. Traditionally, the presidency has been regarded as a relatively unimportant target of group pressure since interest groups only turned to it "as their best medium of expression when they found other pathways blocked." (Bentley, 1908, pp. 344-45) However, such a view is sorely outdated since structural reforms of the presidency itself and changes in its relations with Congress and the bureaucracy have made contacts between the President and interest groups more important for both sides of this relationship.

This essay focuses on relations between the presidency and interest groups during the modern era dating from 1932. After examining changes in the general governmental context, the discussion will concentrate on purposes which Presidents and interest groups pursue through their contacts with each other and the principal channels used for conducting these relations. Finally, we examine possible implications of this network of contacts.

INTEREST-GROUP ACCESS: CONGRESS, BUREAUCRATS, AND THE PRESIDENT

Not all interest groups pursue their collective goals by trying to influence the decisions of public officials. The concerns of some groups, for example, are totally outside the area of public action. Others, however, find it critical to maintain permanent representatives in Washington to influence policymaking and keep their members informed of new developments. This essay focuses on such "political" interest groups, ones which pursue their common interests by attempting to influence the elected or appointed officials who make public policy. Most importantly, interest groups seek access to public officials so that influence can be exerted when necessary. As David Truman explained, "Toward whatever institution of government we observe interest groups operating, the common feature of all their efforts is the attempt to achieve effective access to points of decision." (Truman, 1964, p. 264)

In the scramble for access to national decision-makers, Congress and the bureaucracy have been considered more promising and critical targets than the presidency. In comparison with the President, legislators are selected from a smaller constituency which supposedly makes them more susceptible to group demands. A disgruntled group can have a more direct effect on a congressman's election than on the election of a President whose national constituency dilutes the impact of any single interest. In addition, the legislature's principal responsibility for passing laws makes it appear a more direct route to effect or prevent changes in national policy. Finally, Congress's institutional structure has been considered more decentralized then the presidency's. Numerous committees and elaborate procedures provide countless opportunities for groups to have an impact on legislation.

The executive-branch counterpart to congressional fragmentation is the bureaucracy with its bewildering array of specialized agencies and departments whose employees operate programs with a direct impact on "clientele groups" in the public. For example, the Department of Labor administers programs which deal with workers' health and safety, unemployment insurance, labor-management relations, wage and hour laws, and equal employment opportunity. Clientele groups, in this case organized labor, seek to influence an agency's administrators since they exercise considerable discretion in the operation of programs. In addition, bureaucrats can influence congressional action by recommending new or refined programs and by providing expert testimony on pending legislation.

In contrast to these fragmented, penetrable institutions, the presidency has been portrayed as structurally monolithic, an imposing Everest which is less directly related to either law-making or program administration. Before the New Deal, for example, vigorous presidential support of legislation pending in Congress was not expected. Theodore Roosevelt's and Woodrow Wilson's sponsorship of major programs were considered unusual. The President's importance to interest groups was generally limited to his ability to appoint sympathetic officials to posts in the executive bureaucracy and an occasional exercise of his discretionary powers.

Since the New Deal, a number of changes have made the presidency a more accessible and more significant center of decision-making. Modern Presidents wield much greater influence over legislation, potentially exercise greater control over the executive bureaucracy and receive assistance from hundreds of staffers in dealing with political and policy problems. As a result, interest groups now face a more complex situation in which the presidency's importance has increased without necessarily reducing that of Congress and bureaucrats.

In short, the modern presidency has become a center of power and influence in all phases of the governmental process. Consequently, it has become just as important a target for interest-group lobbying as the Congress or the bureaucracy. Moreover, the vastly expanded modern presidency offers interest groups many more opportunities to gain access to the White House and influence the decision process. Presidents Nixon, Ford, and Carter, for example, assigned White House staff members, *on a full-time basis,* to deal with the concerns of interest groups through an Office of Public Liaison.

WHAT INTEREST GROUPS SEEK FROM PRESIDENTS

Interest groups seek basically the same goals from the presidency as they do from Congress and the bureaucracy: access to the decision process, symbolic recognition of the group's standing in the political system, and active support of the group's specific demands.

Access has traditionally been won through influencing presidential appointments. Interest groups try to ensure that sympathetic administrators will fill positions in executive agencies which have a direct impact on them. Thus, organized labor is concerned with personnel in the Labor Department but also those in the Federal Mediation and Conciliation Service and on the National Labor Relations Board. The latter two agencies are also important for business groups, who are also concerned about the Department of Commerce and Small Business Administration. Groups communicate their preferences to the President as vacancies arise and, of course, are especially concerned at the outset of a new administration when Presidents fill 2,500-3,000 positions. Presidents are also concerned with interest-group recommendations and have established routine procedures for seeking suggestions. By soliciting advice from affected groups, Presidents hope to avoid politically costly struggles during Senate consideration of administration candidates. In addition, Presidents want their appointees to serve as emissaries to various interest groups. The nonacceptability of an appointee would obviously undermine his or her effectiveness in this capacity.

Over time, expectations develop about the qualifications required for particular positions. The secretary of agriculture is usually a Westerner or Mid-Westerner with strong ties to farming. Western ranching interests expect to have a strong voice in the Interior Department. Nonetheless, an agency's clientele is normally diverse rather than uniform which means the President and his personnel assistants must make significant and often delicate choices among contending claims. For example, corporate and family farming are two distinct patterns in American agriculture. Farm interests are even further divided according to commodities. Thus, bargaining over appointments, which is the process of awarding access, can be quite intricate.

New forces can also arise which serve to disrupt many of the existing expectations about appointments to specific positions. In satisfying the expectations of such recently emergent "categorical" groups as blacks, women, and Hispanics, a President may violate those held by traditional "economic" groups, such as business and labor. An even greater potential for conflict is found in the rise of "programmatic" interest groups such as advocates of consumerism and environmental protection whose views on good policy may seriously differ from those of economic groups. While the Agriculture Department may have been established with the explicit purpose of serving farm interests, its programs also affect food prices and quality, major concerns of consumer advocates. Similarly, protection of the environment may conflict with irrigation and land management interests of the ranching and timber industries. Because programs within the Department of Interior affect both sets of interests, presidential appointments may be critical since they affect an agency's program philosophy and exercise of discretion. Thus, the recent rise of new interest groups based on demographic characteristics or policy goals may intensify conflict over appointments.

Interest groups form impressions about an administration's sensitivity to their concerns based on overall appointment patterns as well as individual appointments to specific policymaking positions. The business community, for example, was concerned not only about the Kennedy administration's appointments to positions with specific responsibility for enforcing antitrust legislation, but also about the overall number of prolabor academics placed in more generalized White House positions. They were also aware that far fewer personnel in the Kennedy administration came from commercial backgrounds than had been the case under Eisenhower. (Heath, 1969) The appointment of identifiable members of one's own group seems to have a general "symbolic" significance for many interests. For this reason, Jewish groups reportedly took exception to Nixon's small number of Jewish appointments as well as his failure to appoint anyone to the "Jewish Seat" on the Supreme Court.

Conversely, administration officials like to point proudly to the appointment of a group's members as a way to demonstrate presidential sensitivity to its interests. Thus, President Carter's appeal to Hispanics for reelection support emphasized the appointment of 107 Hispanics to government positions and another 68 to boards and commissions. (Pierce and Hagstrom, *The National Journal*, 1/7/79) Such appeals may be especially significant for groups which have only recently emerged as an organized interest or who perceive themselves as having been excluded from political influence in the past. Jobs, in this case, seem to have especially important symbolic significance.

Symbolic appointments also extend to the White House. Under President Ford, White House assistants for liaison with various groups, such as women, blacks, Hispanics, and youth, were themselves members of the group with which they dealt. Stephen Hess terms this a system of "resident" representation and notes that it was also used during the Johnson administration. Frederick E. Morrow, the first black ever to serve in a White House executive capacity explained, "My position in the White House has been unique. To Negro Americans, I am a symbol of achievement. The Negro press watches every move I make . . . ." (Morrow, 1963, p. 182)

Other presidential practices seem to have symbolic value for interest groups as well. For example, Kennedy elevated the stature of labor in American society by including leaders of prestigious unions on invitation lists for White House functions from which they had been largely excluded by Eisenhower. Similarly, appointment to highly visible, prestigious advisory positions provides recognition for groups as well as their individual leaders. George Meany, former President of the AFL-CIO, served on eight presidential advisory commissions under Presidents Truman, Eisenhower, Kennedy, and Johnson, a symbol of labor's clout as well as that of its leader. Because of the presidency's central position in the American consciousness it is particularly well situated to provide the symbolic recognition which some interest groups demand.

In addition to access and symbolic attention, a President may provide support for the specific policy goals of a group. This may be extended through presidential sponsorship of legislation benefiting the interest or through exercise of executive powers at his discretion. In both cases, interest groups hope to be consulted by an administration before action is taken.

The area of civil rights offers a good example of how Presidents can provide tangible benefits to a group. Presidents Truman, Kennedy, and Johnson had two ways in which they could try to improve the condition of American blacks: sponsoring legislation and using their executive authority. Presidents Kennedy and Johnson adopted the first strategy when they sponsored and fought for the passage of the 1964 Civil Rights Act. On other occasions, Truman and Kennedy made effective use of the second strategy. After encountering opposition to legislation, Truman issued executive orders in 1948 which desegregated the armed forces and sought to reduce discrimination in federal employment and the awarding of government contracts. Initially, Kennedy also relied heavily on executive orders to promote civil rights since it was felt congressional support was too weak to pass major legislation.

Kennedy's actions included use of executive orders to ban discrimination in interstate transportation and the awarding of government contracts; to support special programs for black youths with White House contingency funds; to create the Committee on Equal Employment Opportunity; and to enforce civil rights statutes aggressively. These actions closely paralleled recommendations presented to Kennedy during a January 1961 meeting with civil rights leaders who urged the President-elect to make full use of his executive powers to improve the condition of American blacks. Specific areas of action were identified in an elaborate 61-page memo entitled "Federally Supported Discrimination" given to Kennedy and distributed widely throughout the administration. Roy Wilkins, head of the NAACP and leader of this lobbying effort, suggested that Kennedy's use of executive orders and his sponsorship of what became the 1964 Civil Rights Act could be traced to these presentations. Wilkins also claimed that certain provisions of the act were included by the President only because of pressure from civil rights groups. (Wolk, 1971)

In contrast to Kennedy's personal interaction and extensive consultation with civil rights leaders, Eisenhower's first face-to-face meeting with black leaders did not occur until well into his second term. It can be argued that Kennedy's narrow election victory in 1960 made him susceptible to pressure since blacks gave him valuable voting support and would be needed again in 1964. In contrast, Eisenhower enjoyed wide popularity and had gathered a different electoral coalition making him considerably less sensitive to pressures for action.

On one hand, interest groups use the White House to achieve the "positive" goals of new programs providing benefits and guarantees. They may also seek to defend what they already have against claims of rival interests. The predominantly white New York City building trades unions, for example, found President Nixon to be an important ally in their efforts to resist integration of the construction industry. In the hope of winning union votes, the Nixon administration substantially reduced federal pressure on the unions to hire minorities. A voluntary plan negotiated by the Department of Labor had set a goal of 800 minority trainees by June 1972, but only 203 had been hired by the deadline. The administration delayed a major review of the union's compliance with the agreement, thereby reducing the likelihood of a mandatory integration program. Thus, the union groups achieved a defensive goal through favorable exercise of executive discretion. Election support from the unions was the administration's goal, which takes us to the next topic.

WHAT PRESIDENTS SEEK FROM INTEREST GROUPS

In exchange for helping interest groups, Presidents seek electoral support, assistance in dealing with Congress, and cooperation in the formulation and implementation of policy. Although all three presidential interests are important, most academic and journalistic attention has been devoted to interest groups' electoral significance.

Interest groups can help presidential candidates in a variety of ways. Groups with a sizable membership may be able to deliver a large and cohesive bloc of votes with an important impact on the outcome of primaries (when turnout is low) or the general election (when victory in a few key states with large electoral vote totals is critical). Campaign contributions help candidates meet the "start up" costs of winning the nomination and have been essential to defray the spiraling costs of more sophisticated media campaigns. Interest-group services to presidential candidates include workers to canvass voters, conduct registration drives and transport voters to the polls. A group's bargaining power with the candidate will be increased if support is early or particularly critical to victory.

Campaign practices of the Nixon administration during the 1972 election present all too lurid an illustration of how incumbent Presidents can use their powers to seek interest-group support for their election campaigns. Because of congressional investigations into Watergate and related problems, we have a rather full record of how the Committee to Re-elect the President traded favors for contributions and courted voting blocs through careful targeting of government projects and contracts. Many of the most blatant activities are described in Carol S. Greenwald's book *Group Power* which summarizes much material contained in reports of the Senate Select Committee on Presidential Campaign Activities. These activities may not be typical of other presidential candidates' behavior, but the "inside" look illustrates the range of opportunities available for making deals with interest groups in order to win electoral support.

Perhaps the most infamous trade of policy support for campaign contributions was the Nixon administration's arrangement with the American Milk Producers, Inc. (AMPI) to help secure government policies favorable for their members in exchange for 1970 and 1972 campaign contributions. AMPI's agents struck the bargain through a series of meetings with Nixon representatives and delivered $100,000 for Republican candidates in 1970 and pledged $2 million toward the President's 1972 campaign. Actual AMPI contributions toward the reelection amounted to $632,500. In return, the administration altered its position on federal price supports for milk so that dairymen received $300 million more in 1971 income. (Greenwald, 1977, pp. 3-9)

As a means to win group voting support, the Nixon administration established a system to review government policies, grants, contracts, and personnel appointments in order to maximize their benefit on the President's reelection. The "Responsiveness Program" sought to cultivate support among blacks, Hispanics, the elderly, and labor by providing benefits in a highly selective manner.

Nixon's tactics may have been extreme, but they were not atypical. Groups have traditionally traded election support for access and policy responsiveness. Including a plank in the party's election platform has been a way for presidential candidates to assure groups of a post-election hearing and possible support for a specific set of policy ideas. Interest groups with substantial financial resources have been courted by candidates of both parties to finance campaigns whose total expenditures peaked in 1972 when Nixon and McGovern together spent more than $90 million. Oil companies, for example, have sought to protect their interests by bargaining with presidential candidates who were eager to obtain campaign funds in exchange for promises to support import quotas, the oil depletion allowance, and tax write-offs for drilling costs. Such policy commitments often were made in a personal appearance at the Petroleum Club in Houston to which candidates from both parties traveled. Nixon and Kennedy visited in 1960 and Eugene McCarthy reportedly raised $40,000 in a single day in 1968. Hubert Humphrey and George McGovern were unusual in failing to make the trek. Approximately 10 percent of Nixon's 1972 campaign budget ($5 million) came from oil company officials, stockholders, and corporate funds, the last of which was illegal. (Davis, 1978, pp. 69-72)

Reforms of campaign finance laws passed in 1974 and 1976 may alter this traditional channel of group influence. Limits on individual, group, or corporate contributions, ceilings on candidate spending and a system of enforcement may reduce the significance of interest-group contributions. Candidates for party nominations become eligible for federal matching funds by raising $5,000 in each of 20 states from individual donations limited to $250. Interest-group donations are not matchable during the pre-convention phase and acceptance of federal funds requires that candidates observe spending limits on both national and state campaigns. In addition, nearly full federal funding is available for the November general election which helped to reduce campaign spending in 1976 since both Carter and Ford had to observe limits once they accepted federal funds.

However, reliance on federal funding is optional rather than mandatory. At least one candidate in 1980, Republican John Connally, refused to accept public funding for the nomination stage which allowed him to ignore the spending limitations. Thus, there have been major changes in electoral rules of the game which may reduce the opportunities enjoyed by special interests to influence presidential candidates through contributions. But some uncertainty still remains about the operation of this new system.

Although candidates no longer depend so heavily on interest groups for campaign contributions, voting support remains an important interest group resource. In each of the last three administrations, incumbents ran reelection campaigns from the White House (Nixon, Ford, and Carter) and used staff members in interest-group liaison positions as a means to establish links with group leaders and "sell" the administration's record in meeting group needs. Nixon's liaison staff, headed by Charles Colson, was involved in electoral activity from its inception in November 1969. It regularly intervened in administration policy discussions to point out the political implications of various decisions such as those involving AMPI. Ford's Office of Public Liaison was directed by William Baroody, Jr., Colson's successor. Baroody's staff deemphasized dirty tricks to focus instead on the electoral benefits derived from good public relations. Consequently, it used a soft-sell approach in contrast to Nixon's hard-sell. This unit conducted White House conferences attended by interest-group representatives to discuss major public issues, organized a series of regional town meetings throughout the United States attended by administration officials, and briefed small gatherings of interest-group leaders on administration policies. During 1976, much of the liaison staff was involved in Ford's reelection campaign, but their activity was limited because of sensitivity to Nixon administration improprieties.

Carter initially de-emphasized public liaison and reduced the staff to a bare skeleton under Midge Costanza's direction. However, following a massive erosion of Carter's public support as indicated in the polls a general White House shake-up took place which included Costanza's departure. The public liaison unit was revived in April 1978 under Washington insider Anne

Wexler. The unit has sought to improve the administration's relations with labor, business, environmentalists, urban and suburban interests at least in part because it was recognized that Carter's re-election chances were slim. As a result of Carter's "Rose Garden" campaign strategy of 1979-80, the unit had a prominent election-year role by bringing group leaders to the White House for presidential meetings.

The practice of striking implicit if not explicit bargains with interest groups over campaign support and public policy is likely to continue. Recently, the National Education Association (NEA) endorsed Jimmy Carter for President, something the organization did for the first time in 1976 after candidate Carter promised to establish a separate Department of Education. This executive reorganization passed Congress on September 27, 1979, and the NEA's endorsement for 1980 was announced September 28. In addition to financial and voting benefits which the President is likely to receive, the NEA plays an important role within the Democratic party. Its members comprised the largest single organizational bloc of delegates and alternates at the 1976 convention, (*Congressional Quarterly Weekly Report,* 10/6/79, p. 2209)

In addition to courting interest groups for help in election campaigns, Presidents try to enlist their support in lobbying Congress to pass administration-sponsored proposals. In this way, interest groups become part of a President's "governing coalition." Specialists in congressional relations from executive-branch agencies and the White House obtain valuable information from interest-group lobbyists. White House representatives divide the labor of contacting individual legislators with interest-group spokesmen who often have *better* access to senators or congressmen than do the administration's lobbyists. For example, organized labor received credit for providing much-needed assistance to the Kennedy and Johnson administrations in obtaining passage of New Frontier and Great Society programs.

Anne Wexler's office in the Carter White House has had a very explicit role in seeking to win interest-group support for administration proposals in Congress. As she described the office's purpose in an interview with Dom Bonafede of *National Journal,* " 'Our job is to build an outside coalition for each of the major issues and provide backup' " for the congressional relations staff. (1/13/79, p. 56) By providing information to groups likely to benefit from administration proposals, it is hoped that they will mount additional pressure on Congress. This is an activity performed by previous liaison offices as well, but never in quite so open and organized a fashion. As Wexler put it more directly in a later interview, " 'Our job is to create lobbyists...We do that by educating people on the substance of the issues.' " *(National Journal,* 9/18/79, p. 1476) Even if these efforts do not elicit *active* support, they may prevent group complaints from being voiced in Congress at a later stage.

Carter's liaison operations have been structured differently from those of his two predecessors. Under Nixon and Ford, staff in the public liaison office were assigned to deal with specific constituencies whose interests tended to focus on a relatively narrow range of issues. Under Carter, Wexler's eight full-time aides have specific issue assignments (urban affairs, foreign trade, health policy, regulatory reform/economics, etc.) which might involve contacts with many different groups. However, there are at least seven additional staff members located elsewhere in the White House who focus solely on constituency liaison with significant voting groups: blacks, Jews, women, the elderly, business, consumers, and Hispanics. The result is a more extensive interest-group liaison capability than has ever existed in the White House with one group of staffers focusing on electoral coalitions and the other on governing coalitions. Ironically, it was developed under a President who initially stressed his reluctance to deal with special interests. This change may reflect presidential learning about how to be effective in Washington, desperation over poor reelection prospects, or horrible relations with Congress. Whatever the explanation, Carter, like his predecessors, has learned the importance of interest groups for achieving his electoral and governing purposes.

Governing includes the formulation and implementation of policy. Presidential policymakers need information from affected interest groups on both technical and political matters. Often, a President needs interest-group cooperation in order to have policies actually *work*. Thus, interest groups are very important to a President, not only during an election or in dealing with Congress, but in pursuing the policy goals of the administration as well.

As noted earlier, civil-rights groups could provide the Kennedy administration with an elaborate agenda which served as the basis for executive action and legislative strategies. However, soliciting information is not purely designed to meet the decision needs of policymakers. Interest groups are also consulted as a means to win their active support for or, at a minimum, compliance with administration proposals. Consultation may help avoid opposition expressed in Congress or through some independent action of the interest group designed to combat the administration's purposes. White House liaison staffs have always had the ostensible purpose of *representing* the views of interest groups in the decision-making process; but, as noted earlier, they have had the coordinate purpose of *selling* administration positions to these groups as well.

Interest-group cooperation can be critical to the implementation of administration policies. Involving a group during the decision stage may win later cooperation. At times, Presidents have also sought to prevent groups from doing something which might prove damaging to administration policies. For example, both Presidents Nixon and Eisenhower attempted to dissuade Jewish groups from demonstrating publicly against visiting foreign dignitaries who had offended Israel. They feared such demonstrations might create foreign-policy problems. Nixon dispatched Leonard Garment to head off demonstrations aimed at French President Pompidou. Dwight Eisenhower invited American Jewish leaders to meet with him in the White House in 1960 in hopes of defusing planned action against Egyptian President Nasser who was to visit the United Nations. In both cases, avoiding international embarassment and potential damage to foreign relations could only be achieved through the groups' cooperation. A variation in this pattern occurred in 1975 when action by union members forced the President to modify policy toward the Soviet Union. The International Longshoreman's Association refused to load American grain on Soviet ships which forced the Ford administration to negotiate an agreement with the Russians placing limits on future sales. Details of the agreement were worked out during personal meetings between President Ford, George Meany, and other labor leaders.

Economic policy is a major area in which Presidents are dependent on group cooperation in order to achieve important policy goals. In dealing with business and labor groups, Presidents have few policy tools at their disposal and are limited to "jaw boning," use of threats, and the ability to mobilize public opinion against private interests. A variety of consultation mechanisms have also been used by Presidents to win business and labor support for administration policies. In addition, Presidents have tried to gain group cooperation and allay group fears through personal meetings, public addresses, and symbolic action. Kennedy, for example, attempted to calm business community fears of favoritism toward labor by forming a "neutral" Advisory Committee on Labor-Management Policy with equal representation for business and labor during the first month of his administration. Regular meetings on economic policy were held by a committee which included eight top business executives and Kennedy's Council of Economic Advisers. Kennedy also sponsored legislation favorable to business interests and spoke personally to business audiences. (Heath, 1969)

Nixon sought cooperation from business and labor in administering wage and price controls by appointing representatives from both to the pay and price councils in 1971. Ford established the President's Labor-Management Committee in 1974 which included the corporate chairmen of General Electric, General Motors, First National Citibank as well as the chief officials of the AFL-CIO. Carter's Price Advisory Committee is the most recent effort to seek cooperation from economic groups. This formal mechanism has been supplemented by meetings between the President and business leaders, regular liaison through cabinet members, and full-time White House assistants for business and labor relations.

Thus, Presidents are not passive targets of interest-group activity, rather, they have major purposes to pursue in their dealings with specific interests and have mobilized a variety of resources to help them be successful bargainers.

CHANNELS BETWEEN PRESIDENTS AND INTEREST GROUPS

As suggested in the discussion of goals pursued by Presidents and interest groups, there are a variety of techniques and structures available for maintaining relations between the presidency and specialized publics. Presidents become personally involved in some contacts through appearances at group conventions, private meetings with group leaders to discuss substantive issues or largely ceremonial activities such as the "visitor hours" during which Nixon and Ford received guests in the Oval Office for a handshake, brief chat, photo opportunity, or the presentation of a small memento such as cuff links, golf balls, etc. Direct contact with the President has the advantage of demonstrating his personal awareness of an interest group and its concerns, but involves a heavy commitment in time. In addition, important bargaining discussions with interest groups are perhaps better conducted by intermediaries. Thus, the bulk of interest-group interactions appear to be directed through "presidential surrogates," figures who have ties to the President and serve as emissaries to and from the interest groups.

Although personal friends of the President are sometimes used as emissaries, this task is more often assigned to people holding authoritative positions: administration appointees to the executive bureaucracy, White House staff personnel, or advisory committees whose membership is designed to represent relevant publics. These channels offer a variety of advantages and disadvantages to Presidents and interest groups.

Political appointees in the bureaucracy deal extensively with the clients directly affected by the programs they administer. Thus, there are occasions on which they are called upon to serve as administration representatives to interest groups. However, there is a notorious tendency for executive officials to become advocates of the client groups they serve rather than function as presidential spokesmen. Depending on the outcome of struggles over appointments, bureaucrats often hold the same policy views as their clients and may therefore disagree with specific administration decisions. In addition, administrators often depend on clients for political support in dealing with Congress, particularly over budget matters, or for future personal benefits such as a job at the conclusion of government service. Thus, reliance on bureaucratic channels may favor interest groups over the President in terms of representation of views.

Members of the White House staff may be more effective representatives of presidential stakes in dealing with interest groups because, unlike appointed bureaucrats, they are exclusively responsible to the Chief Executive. Even former members of interest groups seem to move toward the President's point of view after becoming part of the White House system. For example, Carter appointed a founder of the Natural Resources Defense Council (a leading environmental group) to the Council on Environmental Quality, a move which was regarded as providing environmentalists with a favorable voice in administration councils. Even so, the appointee, Gus Speth, reportedly advocated some positions on nuclear power which former associates found inconsistent with his earlier positions. Service in the administration may have presented him with new perspectives on the need to make pragmatic compromises. (*National Journal,* 6/23/79, pp. 1036-39)

White House staff dealing with "political" or constituency liaison tasks provide valuable access points for interest groups to exert influence. But their emergence as a specialized assignment in the White House primarily reflects the benefits they can provide Presidents. For example, Presidents reap some symbolic value from having assistants to serve Hispanics, blacks, Jews, women, business, etc., since each interest may feel someone in the White House is available to listen to its demands. Liaison staffers describe themselves as "lightning rods" since they deflect complaints away from the President and attempt to explain and justify administration programs. They also offer advice on the political ramifications of policy decisions so that mistakes might be avoided.

Despite the fact that White House staff are responsible only to the President, a problem may sometimes arise when staff members face a conflict between loyalty to the administration/President and loyalty to their outside constituencies. Such crises of conscience are most likely to occur when a staff member's personal identity is related to the interest group he serves, and when the group's policy preferences differ from those of the President. Such a situation arose under Carter when Mark Siegel, White House liaison with the Jewish community, resigned in protest over the administration decision to sell jet fighters to Egypt and Saudi Arabia despite Israeli and American Jewish objections. Perhaps the most poignant of these conflicts is described in Frederick Morrow's record of his service in the Eisenhower administration.

> I am an appointee of the Administration, with loyalty to that Administration, to the party and the President, but I am also a Negro who feels very keenly the ills that afflict my race in its efforts to secure in one fell swoop all the privileges and responsibilities of citizenship that have been denied it for three centuries in this country. It is my responsibility to explain to white people how Negroes feel on this matter, and by the same token, explain to Negroes

the Administration's attitude. The time may come when I will find that these two responsibilities are incompatible. (Morrow, p. 48)

In addition to appointed bureaucrats and White House staffers, Presidents have employed a variety of advisory bodies as channels to various interest groups. By establishing a commission, committee, conference, panel, council, or task force to make policy recommendations to the President, the executive indicates his awareness of a problem and signals a disposition to act. There has been considerable disagreement on whether these forums are principally a means to displace group pressure and legitimize past policy or whether they actually formulate innovative programs. Nonetheless, they share the common feature of using committee composition as a way to provide access to groups with direct interest in a special problem. Thomas Wolanin's detailed study of ninety-nine presidential commissions from the period 1945 to 1972 led him to conclude that innovative policies do emerge from such groups and that they also serve as a means to facilitate the adoption of proposals. (Wolanin, 1975) The balance of advantages for the President as compared to the interest group is unclear in these advisory bodies, particularly because they have not been extensively studied. But, insofar as the President controls action taken on recommendations, they must be considered favoring the executive more than the represented groups.

IMPLICATIONS AND EVALUATION

Relations between political interest groups and the American presidency have undergone extensive change in the modern era. While the presidency has become more significant as a decision-making center with a greater impact on group interests, it has simultaneously become more complex and more accessible to group pressures. However, new liaison channels appear to serve *presidential* interests far better than those of the groups they ostensibly represent. What consequences are these changes likely to have? Should they be considered beneficial or detrimental? These questions can be examined from a "pluralist" and from a "corporatist" perspective.

A pluralist view of the new interaction patterns would emphasize *benefits* gained from providing interest groups with expanded opportunities to be heard in presidential decision-making thereby making the executive more like Congress and the bureaucracy. Presentation of group views is considered a legitimate and valuable part of the decision process; like legislators and bureaucrats, presidential staff will find interest-group information important in fulfilling their tasks. In this view, better decisions and greater public participation are positive results likely to flow from recent changes.

Extensive contacts between the presidency and multiple publics may also help to counter tendencies toward presidential isolation and closed decision-making patterns associated with Watergate. Political and social realities may be more easily and effectively conveyed from the outside to the inside of the White House.

In contrast, the corporatist perspective emphasizes *dangers* potentially resulting from closer President-interest-group ties. There is some evidence to indicate that interest groups develop large "umbrella" organizations of national scope in order to deal more effectively with centralized executive authority. Yet, the consequence of this process may well be greater presidential control over interest groups rather than better interest-group representation before the President.

This possible development is all the more ominous if congressional power is indeed declining in the face of executive expansion and political parties continue to suffer an erosion of influence. In such a context, enlarged interest groups would become more and more dependent on a dominant Chief Executive as the legislature and party organizations are relegated to the political background. A dominant executive buttressed by large but dependent national interest groups would become the center of government and politics.

Such a system would be a significant departure from the decentralized *pluralist* pattern of American government and politics. It would come closer to the *corporatist* pattern found in European and South American political systems. It can be argued that the corporatist system allows for more rational policymaking at the national level since the interests of all groups are considered and factored into decision-making by the executive acting as an "honest broker." However, such a system lacks the check on central authority which pluralism provides through fragmented organizational structures and shared governmental authority. It also involves a far different pattern of "representation" than that to which Americans are accustomed.

In conclusion, it is clear that relatiortships between the President and interest groups are dynamic rather than static and are subject to a complex variety of influences. While the post-New Deal patterns identified in this essay may be short-lived, there is the possibility that they could not only alter the process through which decisions are made but also constitute change in fundamental features of the political system.

Suggested Readings

Little attention has been devoted by students of the presidency to relations with interest groups in general. Instead, most discussions of these relationships are found in studies of interest groups such as Carol S. Greenwald, *Group Power: Lobbying and Public Policy*, Praeger, 1977, and the much earlier David B. Truman, *The Governmental Process*, Alfred A. Knopf, 1964. Truman's book is a classic, but somewhat dated while Greenwald presents a wealth of contemporary examples. There are a number of more specific studies focused on relations of one interest group with either a single President or with several Presidents over time. Allan Wolk, *The Presidency and Black Civil Rights: Eisenhower to Nixon*, Fairleigh Dickinson University Press, 1971, adopts the longitudinal approach while Jim F. Heath, *John F. Kennedy and the Business Community*, Chicago University Press, 1969, takes a more short-run focus. Both studies are detailed with the former making more effective use of personal interviews with actual participants. Grant McConnell, *Steel and the Presidency*, W.W. Norton, 1963, adopts a more historical perspective for locating the famous conflict between Kennedy and the steel industry over price increases.

Richard F. Fenno, *The President's Cabinet*, Harvard University Press, 1959, remains the definitive study of this traditional channel between interest groups and the presidency. New perspectives, however, can be found in the work of Thomas Cronin, especially his " 'Everyone Believes in Democracy Until He Gets to the White House. . .': An Examination of White House-Departmental Relations," which has been widely reprinted although it first appeared in *Law and Contemporary Problems*, Vol. 35, no. 3 (Summer 1970). Nelson Polsby has discussed "Presidential Cabinet Making: Lessons for the Political System," in *Political Science Quarterly*, (Spring 1978), in which he links recent changes in presidential elections to new appointment patterns.

A detailed account of several fundamental changes in the modern presidency's structure and institutional relations can be found in Stephen Wayne, *The Legislative Presidency*, Harper and Row, 1978. Thomas R. Wolanin, *Presidential Advisory Commissions*, University of Wisconsin Press, 1975, reviews the operation and effect of these structures from Truman through Nixon, and Samuel I. Doctors and Anne Sigismund Huff, *Minority Enterprise and the President's Council*, Ballinger, 1973, present a detailed account of one advisory body under Nixon.

White House liaison with constituency groups has received little academic attention. Frederick E. Morrow, *Black Man in the White House*, Coward-McCann, 1963, presents an autobiographical account of the first black to serve in an executive capacity in the White House. It is valuable as an "insider's" view of presidential action on civil rights in the 1950s and in portraying the basic activities and potential pressures of the liaison job. Journalistic accounts of the liaison staff are more numerous with Dom Bonafede's excellent articles in the *National Journal* being the best. They can be found in issues on the following dates: 9/8/79; 1/13/79; 1/24/76; 9/8/70. In addition, *National Journal* carries in-depth articles on specific interest-group communities which have been referred to in the essay itself.

Other References Cited

Arthur F. Bentley, *The Process of Government*, Chicago University Press, 1908.

David Howard Davis, *Energy Politics*, 2nd ed., St. Martin's, 1978.

"FORWARD ON THE FOE!!"

The President and Political Parties

Joseph Parker and Edward N. Kearny

University of Southern Mississippi
and Western Kentucky University

The United States Constitution allocates a burdensome array of duties to the President, but it does not impose upon him the task of political party leadership. This role as party leader was added to the presidency after its creation and in many ways does not fit comfortably with many of the roles of the President. The framers of the Constitution were disdainful of political parties as divisive forces which would undermine national unity and be destructive of national well-being. They sought to create a presidential office which would not depend upon parties in the choice of a President and a presidency that would not depend upon parties as a vehicle for the achievement of policy goals while in office. In short, they believed in an "apartisan presidency"; an office which would steadfastly keep its distance from any factions or parties which might develop in the new nation.

Washington was able to live up to the apartisan presidential role envisioned by the authors of the Constitution in a way that no other President has. Though political parties emerged in embryonic form during Washington's presidency, they took form largely in voting patterns in Congress and in congressional elections. He kept his distance from these young parties and rejected a direct partisan role as incompatible with his concept of the office. Partisan maneuvering was left to Washington's trusted deputy, Alexander Hamilton.

The genuine father of the role of the President as party leader is Thomas Jefferson who, with the able assistance of James Madison, built the first national political party as an instrument of peaceful opposition to the government in power. He used this invention of his fertile mind as an election vehicle for his pursuit of the presidency in 1800. In the space of twelve short years the apartisan presidency which the framers of the Constitution had gone to such pains to create had been converted into a partisan presidency. Yet, as we shall see later, the notion of an apartisan presidency (the Washingtonian Model) has remained a firmly established ideal and in certain situations a wise political approach for a President.

For Jefferson the partisan presidency was richly rewarding. He continued his role as party leader once in office, and subsequent Presidents have done so as well. Even Presidents like Eisenhower, who had little taste for partisan politics, have had the party leadership role thrust upon them. Mr. Jefferson was able to rely upon his party loyalists in Congress to get legislation passed. In fact, for Jefferson the party was such a reliable instrument of power that only on a few occasions did he need to stretch the powers of his office. The assessment of his presidency has generally been that he was a strong President who weakened the presidential office. Most Presidents have not enjoyed Jefferson's good fortune in reaping rich dividends from party leadership.

The modern presidency represents something of a blending of the Washingtonian and Jeffersonian models in dealing with political parties. The President is much more entangled with his political party and assumes much more of a party leadership role than the Founding Fathers would have wished. Yet, he is much less a party leader and is far more independent of his political party for support than was Thomas Jefferson.

This mixture of partisan and apartisan elements in the modern presidency varies with the different phases of seeking and conducting the office. The partisan element is highest when a presidential aspirant or an incumbent seeks the nomination or renomination of his party. It generally declines significantly after the aspirant or incumbent has been nominated and begins to seek the support of independent voters and those who are weakly attached to the opposing party. Partisanship declines still further after the election when the task of governing begins. Modern Presidents in their pursuit of both public and congressional support have found it necessary to stand above narrow partisanship. Advances in communications instruments such as television have given both Presidents and presidential candidates alternatives to the political party in taking their case to the American electorate. *The Nature of Parties in the United States.* The role of the President as party leader is set upon a shaky foundation. American parties are decentralized structures that make the President's leadership role extremely difficult. According to a leading presidential scholar, Louis W. Koenig:

> The local and state party organizations are beyond his control and are subject, at most, to his influence. The major parties function as viable national organizations only quadrennially, when their state and local parts more or less unite to win the presidency and its stakes of power. Thereafter the parts conduct themselves with jealously preserved autonomy.

With their decentralized organization, national political parties are extremely weak support systems for Presidents attempting to lead in the modern era.

THE PRESIDENTIAL-PARTY CONNECTION

Seeking the Nomination: Maximum Dependence on Party. The connection between a President and his party begins long before he becomes President. Since the emergence of political parties in the United States, all Presidents have been nominated for the office by one of the two major parties. On only a couple of occasions has a third party candidate had a ghost of a chance at election as President. In all but a few instances the candidate must develop strong ties within his party. He may have held a leadership position in his party's national, state, or local organizations; he may have campaigned tirelessly for fellow partisans running for office; he may have cultivated party contacts in his own behalf for years; or he may have done a combination of these things. The cultivation of party ties in pursuit of the presidential nomination has become so time consuming in the last decade that a number of successful candidates, including Jimmy Carter in 1976 and Ronald Reagan in 1980, have done this virtually as a full-time occupation.

In recent times, there has been only one glaring exception. Dwight Eisenhower did not even reveal his party preference until shortly before his nomination by the Republican Party in 1952. He had, in fact, been urged by a diverse group of leading Democrats in 1948 to accept the nomination of their party and there has been a great deal of informed speculation that the nomination would have been his for the asking. Eisenhower gracefully turned his Democratic suitors away in 1948 but did not reveal any affection for the Republican Party. Ike is the rare exception that proves the rule. Most politicians who set their sights on the White House spend years of prodigious work cultivating support in their party.

John F. Kennedy, for example, worked diligently on behalf of the Stevenson-Kefauver Democratic ticket in 1956. Kennedy, who had clearly taken aim on his party's 1960 nomination, campaigned in 24 states, traveled 30,000 miles and made 150 speeches in support of the party nominees. Over the next few years Kennedy traveled to every state in the Union campaigning and raising money on behalf of fellow Democrats. The Kennedy example points up the advantages of actual party service to an aspirant for the presidential nomination. The candidate proves his love of and dedication to party, gains recognition, plants the seeds of an organization, and develops his campaigning skills.

Like Kennedy, Richard Nixon understood that the road to the presidential nomination can be paved with tireless party service. For a full decade prior to receiving the Republican nomination in 1960, Nixon was an energetic campaigner for numerous Republican office seekers. After losing the presidential election in 1960, he was able to capture the Republican nomination for a second time eight years later. Tireless service to party was an indispensable part of his comeback. In 1964, for example, he campaigned in thirty-six states over a six-week period for Barry Goldwater, the Republican candidate for President.

In 1980, George Bush and Ronald Reagan emerged as the strongest contenders for the Republican nomination. Bush had been very active in party affairs, serving as the chairman of the Republican National Committee in 1973-74. Reagan, who captured the nomination, had been an active participant in national Republican Party politics since 1964, and achieved something close to celebrity status among the party faithful as a contender for the presidential nomination in 1968 and 1976.

Two "accidental Presidents," Lyndon Johnson and Gerald Ford, can be viewed as partial exceptions which underscore the rule about the importance of strong party ties in gaining presidential nominations. The political roots of both men were planted much more deeply in Congress than in their national parties (although both were party leaders *in Congress,* they were not very active in national party affairs outside that body).

They first attained the presidency, not by being nominated for that office by their respective parties, but by holding the office of Vice-President when the incumbent President died (Kennedy) or resigned (Nixon) while in office.

Partly because of their relatively shallow party roots, both men lost touch with important ideological segments of their parties. In Johnson's case, strong opposition from within the Democratic Party was a factor in his decision to retire from the presidency rather than seek his party's renomination in 1968. Similarly, Gerald Ford almost lost his bid for the Republican nomination to Ronald Reagan in 1976 even though he was the in-cumbent Republican President.

From these examples, it is clear that in gaining nomination or renomination, the presidential aspirant is heavily dependent on his party. This dependence is reduced to a considerable extent after he gets the nomination and approaches his next hurdle, the general election.

The General Election. There are a number of reasons why a presidential candidate is less dependent on his party at this phase of the selection process. First, once he is nominated, sources of support outside the party become available to him. Most im-portant, simply by being the nominee of one of the two major parties, most of his general election campaign expenses are paid for by the federal government—provided he keeps his overall cam-paign spending within the prescribed federal limits ($29.4 million for each candidate in 1980).

Secondly, in the general election, the candidate cannot rely on the support of his fellow party members alone. He must reach out for support from the large and growing block of independent voters (approximately 32 percent of the electorate as compared to only 21 percent Republicans and 47 percent Democrats)* as well as dissatisfied members of the opposition party.

The disparity between the candidate's heavy dependence on the party during the nomination phase and his greater need for independence from the party during the general election

*Gallup Poll, reported in New Orleans Times *Picayune,* 4/27/80.

phase creates a dilemma for a presidential aspirant whose strategy is to attract broad national support, not only to win the general election, but to govern effectively afterward.

The candidate's dilemma is this: To get the nomination, he must narrow his appeal to the beliefs of those within his own party. He must placate groups of party activists whose opinions on issues are often far removed from the center of national public opinion, yet whose influence within the party is great.

If he tries to broaden his appeal to reach the general electorate before his nomination, he may lose the support of party activists and the nomination along with it. However, if he yields too much to the party activists in his stands on issues, he may become less appealing to moderate and independent voters outside his party, thus inspiring less confidence among voters in the general election.

Many political observers believe that the presidential candidate's dilemma has become more difficult in the past two decades due to the fact that issue-oriented activists have become more powerful in both parties and less inclined to allow their party nominee flexibility in moderating his position on issues in order to appeal to the general electorate. As we have mentioned, Gerald Ford almost lost the Republican nomination in 1976 even though he was an incumbent Republican President. This was because his conduct of the presidency strayed too far from the strong conservative orthodoxy of party activists led by Ronald Reagan.

Jimmy Carter attained the Democratic nomination in 1976 without destroying his national appeal by an unusual ability to devise delicately crafted moderate positions on a number of controversial issues in such a way as not to give too great offense to party activists. Even this skill might not have sufficed had not the Democrats, only four years before, suffered a landslide defeat by nominating the champion of the new party activists, George McGovern.

Ford's near overthrow and Carter's need for unusually careful political footwork in 1976 both attest to the fact that a candidate's shift from the highly partisan demands of the nomination process to the less partisan demands of the general election is a very difficult one to make.

After the Election: Governing the Nation. When the President assumes office, the forces leading him to be "above party," as the

Founders hoped he would be, become much stronger. Indeed, by making the separation of powers a guiding principle of the national government, they left a legacy which has permanently impaired the President's ability to govern the nation effectively by being a strong and effective party leader.

The framers of the Constitution carefully separated the two elected branches of the national government (the presidency and Congress) giving each its own independent source of power in separate elections.

The President may be nominated as the leader of his party, and then elected, thereby demonstrating that the general public prefers him to the leader of the other major party. But his status as the leader of the party which won the presidential election has no binding effect whatsoever on the Congress. The Congress may well be controlled by the other party. President Eisenhower during most of his presidency, and Presidents Nixon and Ford during all of theirs, faced a Congress controlled by the opposition party. In such a situation, the President must play down his position as party leader and rise "above party" to gain the support he needs to lead Congress and the nation.

If the President's party controls both houses of the Congress, his fortunes improve, but not dramatically. Congressmen are proud to belong to a separate and independent branch of government, and do not like to be seen as "rubber stamps" for the President, even if he is the leader of their party. Moreover, the congressman is usually expected to look after the local interests he represents while the President is given more responsibility for the national interest. Thus, there are built-in sources of conflict between the presidency and Congress, even if both are controlled by the same party.

For these reasons, the separation of powers seriously weakens the President's ability to use his status as victorious party leader as a tool to carry out his election campaign promises. A number of scholars have been critical of the limits placed on strong party leadership by our system of government. In the spirit of Thomas Jefferson, they have argued that party leadership by the President should be strong enough to overcome the barriers created by the separation of powers. Only through strong party leadership which is binding on the Congress can the public hold the President and his party responsible for what the government does.

To achieve this end, scholar-reformers have proposed a number of changes which would place congressmen under an obligation to follow party positions stated in their party's platform or enunciated by the President as party leader (if he belongs to the same party as they do). Failure to meet this obligation would result in the loss of a number of desirable privileges in Congress, or even renomination by the party in the next election.

The attempts of scholar-reformers to strengthen the President's hand as a party leader and to bring about "responsible party government" have made little headway against the Founding Fathers' legacy of separation of powers. A number of factors have been responsible for this. Perhaps the most basic cause for failure is that American voters, who are the intended beneficiaries, do not seem to desire these changes.

Quite the contrary, voters take full advantage of the opportunities which the separation of powers system affords them without being very much disturbed by the confusion and contradictions which often result. Voters, for example, show an increasing tendency to vote for a President belonging to one of the major parties and a Congressman who belongs to the other. Similarly, citizens may vote in the same election for a presidential candidate who vows to fight inflation and big government *and* for a Congressman who has a good record of procuring generous amounts of federal programs and benefits for them (which may increase both bureaucracy and inflation).

Under these circumstances, Presidents have no choice but to de-emphasize their party leadership role while governing the nation. If they are to have any success operating in a system of separation of powers, they must reach out to members of the opposition party for support on key issues. They must also be very attentive to the local concerns of congressmen which have little to do with the national party or its platform.

Despite the considerations which force the President in many situations to be "above party," he cannot escape party pressures or his party leadership role. The reasons for the partisan pressures are reasonably obvious. First, the President's need for renomination and reelection depends upon continuing party support. Too much cozying up to the opposition party and too little attention to the demands of the party faithful are likely to make for a one-term presidency. Secondly, the support of *most* of the President's fellow party members in Congress *most* of the time is a necessary, if not sufficient, ingredient of his national leadership. In short, even in the governing stage when apartisan pressures are the strongest, the President is still far more involved in party responsibilities than the Founding Fathers ever intended him to be.

PARTISAN RESPONSIBILITIES OF THE PRESIDENT

Patronage. Once a successful campaign for the White House has been waged, a President will face sizable demands from the party which nominated and elected him for a return upon that investment. There are appointments to positions in his new administration, judicial posts to be filled, invitations to inaugural activities, plus other opportunities to repay some of those party faithful who were most helpful in bringing him to power. The vast extension of the civil service merit system has lessened both the opportunity and the burden of the President in rewarding the faithful. Still, a modern President can count on a vast number of his fellow partisans beating a path to his door in search of a patronage reward for what they claim was an indispensable role in his election. Patronage is often more of a burden than a blessing to the President. By filling an office, he pleases some in his party, but may anger others who thought they, or one of their friends, deserved the job. Presidents must often appoint people who are really the choices of powerful congressmen belonging to the President's party. Here again, the President may make more congressmen angry (because their candidate was not chosen) than grateful. Some observers have even suggested with sarcasm that patronage responsibilities are so troublesome that they should be given to the losers, not the winners, of presidential elections.

Once a newly elected President passes the period of staffing his administration, he settles into a variety of party leadership responsibilities. Unlike the patronage demands which die off generally after the first few months of office, the other demands persist throughout his administration.

Fund Raising. Fund raising is a constant demand upon a President. In the case of the Democratic Party there always seems to be a debt to pay off. During the course of his administration a President is much in demand to appear at fund raising affairs or to provide members of his family and cabinet for such activities. The appearance of the President, his wife, or a prominent cabinet member greatly enhances the prospects for the sale of tickets for party fund-raisers. Presidents generally look upon fund raising as one of the most burdensome and distasteful of their partisan duties, but one which they have great difficulty avoiding.

Campaigning. Campaigning is another partisan expectation of a President, especially if he enjoys strong popularity. A President is generally expected to campaign for congressmen of his party in "off year" elections which occur midway between presidential election contests. Of course, a President cannot campaign for all the candidates of his party. He must make decisions as to where to concentrate his campaign efforts. In many cases he chooses to campaign on behalf of party incumbents who are thought to be in tough reelection fights. In some instances he chooses to campaign for challengers against incumbents of the other party who have been particularly intense in their opposition to his programs. A skillful President will choose carefully among the hundreds of congressional contests, picking those where a party victory will also significantly increase his strength in Congress.

On rare occasions an incumbent President can be sufficiently confident of reelection that he can gear his campaign efforts to provide maximum assistance for his party cohorts running for Congress. Such a situation existed in 1964 when public opinion polls assured President Johnson that a loss to his unpopular opponent would be "the biggest upset since Moses rolled back the Red Sea." Johnson concluded that he could afford to choose states in which to campaign for President with the clear objective of assisting Democrats in tight congressional races. The payoff was a tremendous coattail effect for the Democrats in congressional, state, and local elections. A similar opportunity was presented to Richard Nixon in 1972. However, Nixon largely confined himself to the White House and made virtually no effort on behalf of his fellow Republicans. Though Nixon scored a massive election victory, there was no spin-off benefit for other Republicans. Some Republicans complained that the White House had assured them that if they asked for presidential help it would come when requested. But when requests came, they were ignored. It is not surprising that many Republicans felt no inclination to extend themselves on behalf of Nixon when the Watergate scandal threatened to end his presidency within two years of his landslide victory.

It should be recognized that Presidents are not always an asset to their fellow party members seeking election or reelection. A President riding the crest of public support in the opinion polls can expect to be inundated with requests for campaign appearances while one whose popularity is at a low ebb will find that congressmen of his party prefer that he not come into their districts or states to campaign for them.

Recruiting. It might seem logical that the President as party leader would have a substantial role in recruiting and selecting the candidates who will run for elective office under the party banner. While logical, it is not political reality. The decentralized nature of American political parties is such that party candidates are chosen by state and local party processes which operate more or less independently of the President's wishes. Where the President plays a role, discretion dictates that it be a subtle one. A classic example of the limits of a President's influences on the selection of his party's candidates at the state and local level is Franklin Roosevelt's effort in the 1938 congressional elections to defeat a number of incumbent Democrats in the nominating primaries. On his "hit list" were party cohorts who had consistently opposed his New Deal legislative programs. Roosevelt suffered a humiliating defeat on this occasion, as almost all of the Democrats he sought to purge won renomination with ease.

However, a President can exert some influence on the recruitment of party candidates if he does not use a heavy hand with state and local party leaders. Eisenhower in 1954 through gentle persuasion convinced John Sherman Cooper, then Ambassador to India, that he should seek a United States Senate seat from Kentucky. Cooper was elected in 1954 and distinguished himself in the Senate after his election. In this case, Eisenhower was supporting local Republican leaders, who wanted Cooper to run rather than opposing them, as Roosevelt had done with local Democrats in 1938.

Perhaps the most positive role that a President can and does play in candidate recruitment is to assure a prospective and desirable party candidate for Congress that, if he loses, he will be offered an administration job as a reward for running. The situation which best accommodates itself to this effort is where a party incumbent in the House of Representatives is being urged to run against an incumbent United States senator from the opposition party with only long-shot prospects of defeating him.

Conventional political wisdom dictates that a congressman should not give up a safe seat in the House of Representatives for a less than fifty-fifty chance of gaining a seat in the Senate. Yet it is painful to party leaders, the President included, to see incumbents in the opposition party win a Senate seat unopposed. In 1970, during Nixon's presidency, Rep. Clark McGregor opposed Senator Hubert Humphrey in Minnesota and Rep. Richard Roudebush opposed Senator Vance Hartke in Indiana. Both were long-shot candidates and both were defeated. Shortly after their defeat, however, both received appointments in the Nixon administration. It seems a safe bet that both had been assured a consolation prize before undertaking uphill Senate campaigns against popular incumbents of the opposition party.

Peacemaking. Within many, if not most, state political parties there are frequent disputes and splits between various party factions. These factions may quarrel about political beliefs, patronage, race/ethnicity, or personalities. Whatever their cause, these disputes are generally festering if they have not already erupted. Since governors, United States senators, and other party leaders are frequently allied with one of the factions, they are in a poor position to mediate internal bickering. It often becomes the President's job to be the referee from the outside who plays the peacemaker role. One version of the purpose of John Kennedy's fatal visit to Texas in November 1963 was that it was designed to patch up an internal party squabble between the conservative and liberal wings of the Texas Democratic Party. The other cited purpose was fund raising for the 1964 presidential campaign. It is probable that JFK was doing a bit of both peacemaking and fund raising, both of which he regarded as part of his role as party leader.

Support of Party Machinery. David Broder in *The Party's Over* (1971) makes a strong case for maintaining strong parties in a democracy and for reviving these generally neglected political institutions. No single person in the nation can be more effective in providing the needed support for a major political party than the President. He is the titular, and potentially real, leader of his party. The President's party needs an effective national chairman and the President makes the choice of a chairman. Once chosen, the national chairman requires the cooperation of the President and his White House staff in the task of making the party a vital political force.

Presidents are not always attentive to party needs. Presidential staff personnel frequently see the national chairman and his staff as competitors for presidential attention and sometimes react by denying them access to the President. An example of this situation occurred during Richard Nixon's presidency. Senator Robert Dole who served as Republican national chairman during the 1972 presidential campaign indicated that he had virtually no communications with the President during that election year. On the other hand, John F. Kennedy is frequently cited as a modern President who gave more careful attention than most to nurturing the strength and vitality of his party's national organization. Presidents differ in terms of how much, or how little, interest they take in the health and vitality of their national party organizations.

Policy and Party. A President may affect the health and vitality of his political party much more profoundly by the broad policy and political decisions he makes in office than by the direct interest he takes, or fails to take, in his party's daily or yearly operations.

For example, Franklin D. Roosevelt's bold economic policies during the Great Depression made the Democratic Party the nation's majority party for more than two generations. Lyndon Johnson's unpopular course in Vietnam led to national discontent that contributed to a loss of fifty Democratic seats in the 1966 congressional elections, and the loss of the presidency in 1968. Moreover, the deep divisions spawned within the Democratic Party by Vietnam continued to weaken it long after Johnson left office in 1968.

Richard Nixon's prolonged involvement in the Watergate scandals did great damage to his political party. In 1974, the year he resigned from the presidency in disgrace, the Republicans lost forty-six seats in Congress. Perhaps one of the many reasons why political parties have declined in power and prestige over the last two decades is that neither party has produced a President who, on leaving office, was perceived as reasonably successful since John F. Kennedy was assassinated in 1963.

OUTLOOK FOR THE EIGHTIES

Obviously a President must balance his responsibility as party leader with a variety of other important nonpartisan responsibilities. In many instances his activities as chief Democrat or Republican may make it difficult for him to be accepted as President of all the people or in gaining bipartisan support in Congress for crucial legislative programs.

Joseph A. Califano, Jr., however, takes an extreme view of the extent to which partisanship is a liability to modern Presidents in his book *A Presidential Nation:*

> The political party is at best of marginal relevance to the performance of the duties of the Oval Office. The partisan political allegiance. . . becomes an impediment to those incumbents who aspire to conduct a great presidency. . . irrelevant and ineffective as an instrument to extend the reach of presidential power. (pp. 146-147)

Califano cites Eisenhower, Kennedy, Johnson, and Nixon as Presidents who downplayed party affiliation after election. In Eisenhower's case, he wearied of dealing with Republican neanderthals in the Congress who regarded his progressive Republicanism as something akin to heresy. Ultimately, Eisenhower enjoyed greater legislative success with a Democratic majority in each chamber of Congress than he did when his own party controlled Congress.

Califano contends that Kennedy, Johnson, and Nixon neutralized the role of their party's national committees by shifting significant political decision making to the White House staff and by leaving the national committee as a hollow shell useful only for certain forms of political hack work unbecoming to the Oval Office. Califano contends that the modern presidency must be an apartisan presidency. In Congress, for example, he argues that Presidents cannot count on party majorities. Rather, they need "liberal, conservative, or ad hoc majorities. They need shrewd and well-respected floor managers . . . from either (or both) sides of the aisle." (p. 154) Califano goes on to cite the necessity of opposition party support on certain legislative initiatives by recent Presidents. While his thesis has considerable merit, it has been pointed out earlier in this esssay that *the nucleus of legislative support on most presidential initiatives in recent decades has been the members of the President's party in Congress.* While Califano and others rightly point to such examples as Senate Republican Leader Everett Dirkson's crucial support of President Lyndon Johnson's civil rights proposals, it is equally true that, generally speaking, Dirkson opposed LBJ more frequently than he supported him, and that his support was crucial on the civil-rights measures only because Democrats supplied *almost enough votes* for passage of those pieces of legislation. Califano makes his strongest case in his contention that party leadership must compete with other more potent demands upon the President's time and energy:

> Since . . . Roosevelt, American presidents have been consumed with apparently intractable problems . . . . The incumbent years of a president are aimed at the stuff of history—winning wars, achieving peace, ending depression, harnessing inflation, or wiping out poverty—and reinvigorating partisan political parties is not presidentially perceived as historically momentous. (pp. 159-160)

One might also mention other factors contributing to an apartisan presidency: the reduced need for party fund-raising with publicly financed election campaigns and the reduced need for party workers with television as the major means of communications between presidential candidates and voters.

Despite all of the clear indications that the apartisan presidency may be gaining momentum, the traditional partisan duties of the President will remain. This is true because Presidents need political parties for too many things and therefore cannot afford to conduct their office completely "above party." Most of all, they need their parties as vehicles for nomination and, to a lesser extent, for election. Once elected, they need the support of most of their party cohorts in Congress most of the time. If they lose this nucleus of support, a barely manageable Congress becomes a completely unmanageable Congress and their leadership will collapse. So it seems likely that the apartisan spirit of the Founding Fathers and the partisan spirit of Thomas Jefferson will cohabit the presidency uneasily but indefinitely into the 1980s.

Suggesting Readings

Asher, Herbert. *Presidential Elections and American Politics.* Homewood, Ill.: The Dorsey Press, 1980.

Broder, David. *The Party's Over.* New York: Harper and Row, 1971.

Burns, James MacGregor. *Presidential Government: The Crucible of Leadership.* Boston: Houghton Mifflin Company, 1965.

Burns, James MacGregor. *The Deadlock of Democracy: Four Party Politics in America.* Englewood Cliffs: Prentice-Hall, Inc., 1963.

Califano, Joseph A., Jr. *A Presidential Nation.* New York: W.W. Norton & Company, Inc., 1975.

Koenig, Louis W. *The Chief Executive,* 3rd ed. New York: Harcourt, Brace, Jovanovich, Inc., 1975. Chapter 6.

Sickels, Robert J. *Presidential Transactions.* Englewood Cliffs: Prentice-Hall, Inc., 1974. Chapter 1.

Sorauf, Frank J. *Political Parties in the American System,* 3rd ed. Boston: Little, Brown and Company, 1980.

Wayne, Stephen J. *The Road to the White House: The Politics of Presidential Elections.* New York: Saint Martin's Press, 1980.

Witcover, Jules. *Marathon: The Pursuit of the Presidency 1972-1976.* New York: The Viking Press, 1977.

White, Theodore H. *The Making of the President 1960.* New York: Atheneum House, Inc., 1961.

White, Theodore H. *The Making of the President 1964.* New York: Atheneum House, Inc., 1965.

White, Theodore H. *The Making of the President 1968.* New York: Atheneum House, Inc., 1969.

White, Theodore H. *The Making of the President 1972.* New York: Atheneum House, Inc., 1973.

Presidential Nominations and Elections

Joel Goldstein
University of Louisville

The 1980 presidential election is now history. Many Americans will spend the next four years deciding whether they made the best choice in the primary or caucus voting as well as in the general election. This essay will not delve into the personalities and issue positions of the presidential aspirants who survived the struggle for their party's nomination, but rather examine the system which produced the choice.

The primary function served by the presidential selection process is to select the best individual for the presidency. A secondary function is to provide the newly elected President with the broad national support necessary to govern effectively. In addition, the presidential selection process ought to create a vehicle for the discussion of national issues, so that the electorate can have an impact on the development of national public policy. The effectiveness of the current system to meet these goals has been seriously questioned.

Students of the presidency have often noted that the "best" people are generally not elected President. Henry Clay, Daniel Webster, Robert Taft, and the other "giants" of the Senate during the nineteenth and early twentieth centuries have consistently failed to win the big prize. In addition, with the exceptions of Wendell Wilkie and Dwight Eisenhower, the major party candidates for the presidency during the past half century have come from the political sphere without any serious consideration given to the leaders of the business, labor, or intellectual communities.

A second line of criticism revolves around the argument that the presidential selection process tends to weaken the ability of the President to govern. Presidential leadership has been eroded by the large number of members of the Senate and House of Representatives who are seeking to build a national constituency for their bid for the White House. Most of these leaders act upon the assumption that the best way of building their name recognition and national support is to offer an alternative to the President's policies.

Moreover, the formal campaign for President in 1980 started over a year before the actual election. In comparison, the average Western parliamentary system has an electoral campaign which lasts only six to eight *weeks*. Many critics note that the campaign tends to be characterized by the opponents of the President, both inside and outside his party, criticizing the administration and its policies. In addition, the President tends to spend an inordinate amount of his time campaigning for reelection and worrying about the short-term political ramifications of his decisions rather than governing the nation. President Carter during the first months of 1980 decided to cancel debates scheduled with his opponents for the Democratic nomination so that his attention would not be shifted from the Iranian and Afghanistan crises, yet he did spend several hours on the phone seeking support in the early caucus and primary states.

The presidential campaign, in other words, serves to accentuate the divisions between the executive and legislative branches and to highlight the "nonresponsible" and leaderless character of the American political parties. Neither quality increases the ability of the President to focus public opinion and to lead the Congress into adopting his or her legislative program.

The presidential campaign and its coverage by the electronic and print media have been criticized because of their alleged failure to develop the important issues of the campaign. The media have been accused of focusing in on the "horse-race" aspect of the campaign (who is ahead in state X, which candidate is building momentum, what is the influence of the results of the first caucuses in Iowa and Maine and the opening primary in New Hampshire on the rest of the race, or how the candidates are doing in the Gallup and Harris Polls). The media have also been accused of overemphasizing the personalities behind the presidential campaign (the political headlines during the week following the New Hampshire primary, for example, were dominated by the "reorganizations" within the Reagan and Kennedy camps and the *Today Show* had a series of segments on the candidates' wives) rather than exploring the candidates' positions on the major issues facing the nation.

It is extremely difficult for the electronic media to cover a detailed position paper on a major issue in a forty-five second to two minute spot on the evening news. Consequently, the public's perception of the campaign tends to center on the candidates' image and the "mood" of the electorate. Jimmy Carter's 1976 campaign focused upon the "anti-Washington" mood of the nation.

The presidential selection process has undergone a number of changes. However, there have been only two changes in the constitutional rules governing the selection mechanism itself. The Twelfth Amendment required electors to cast separate ballots for President and Vice-President while the Twenty-second Amendment limited the number of terms a President can serve to two. However, there have been many changes in the way the game is played. Both major parties have modified their rules in response to challenges from within the party. In addition, the environment within which the presidential election takes place has changed. These changes have been due to technological advances as well as modifications in the laws governing the process. There have also been changes in the nature of the electorate and the party structure. This essay will assess these developments in terms of whether or not they advance the goals of the selection process.

TECHNOLOGICAL CHANGES

The style of American presidential politics has changed dramatically since Warren G. Harding was able to spend the 1920 campaign on the front porch of his home at 380 Mount Vernon Avenue, Marion, Ohio. There have been three major changes in technology which have resulted in extensive modifications in the ways presidential campaigns are conducted. The first involves alterations in the modes of transportation. The second, in the way ideas and messages are transmitted across the nation. The third, in the way information is processed.

The jet plane has enabled a presidential contender to travel across the length and breadth of the nation not just once or twice during the last few months of the campaign but almost daily. A typical campaign swing might include visits to New York, Pittsburgh, Cleveland, Chicago, St. Louis, Portland, San Francisco, Los Angeles, Dallas, New Orleans, and Atlanta. A campaign trip like this could take three or four days with the candidate making a major appearance in each city.

A campaign visit of this type serves several purposes. It gives the candidate additional exposure in the local media. The national news coverage a candidate receives is generally independent of the location of the news, but the local coverage certainly is not. Consequently, the stop will increase interest in the campaign and help rally the spirits of the local campaign staff.

Secondly, a visit to a specific city allows the candidate the opportunity to talk about the issues which are of special interest to that area. A speech in the far Northwest would be appropriate for a discussion of conservation while a trip to Harlem would be a good opportunity to deal with the issues of civil rights.

The physical and mental stress placed on the candidate by this type of campaign allows the voters an opportunity to measure whether an individual can withstand the pressures of the presidency. A similar "campaign as a simulation of the presidency" argument can be used to justify the microscopic examinations which the press gives the candidates for President and Vice-President.

The jet airplane changed the pace of the campaign, but it also resulted in a reduced opportunity for small town, rural America to personally see and hear the presidential candidates. The old campaign trains brought the campaign to these cities and towns and gave the residents a change to be close to the nominees. Television is now the vehicle which brings the campaign to these people's homes.

NATIONALIZED MEDIA: TRANSMITTING THE MESSAGE

Presidential campaigns, like many aspects of American life, have been transformed by the advances in communications technology. Half a century ago, citizens learned of the presidential campaign from their local newspapers. In the nineteenth century these were primarily party organs which transmitted the party dogma to the citizenry.

National weekly news magazines like *Time, Newsweek,* and *U.S. News and World Report* now provide millions of Americans their information about the trends of American politics. The coverage of national politics in local newspapers generally comes from the two wire services and the news services of the *New York Times, Washington Post,* and *Los Angeles Times.* The development of these print media institutions resulted in an increased importance for the ideas and perceptions of a few leading reporters. For example, R. W. Apple of the *New York Times,* David Broder of the *Washington Post* and Walter Mears of the Associated Press are now able to strongly influence the national perceptions of what is happening in national politics.

The second major revolution in the media resulted from the development of radio and television news. The network nightly news programs provide almost every American with a common source of information. The attention paid to the results of the party caucuses and primaries by the print and electronic media can transform an individual from a position in the middle of the pack to a leading contender for the nomination almost overnight. The February 4, 1980, *Newsweek,* for example, reported that George Bush moved from a 6 percent portion of the Republican preference for the party nomination to 27 percent in the ten days sandwiched around the Iowa caucus results. John Anderson's meteoric rise in the polls following his success in Massachusetts is another example from the 1980 elections. Jimmy Carter's 1976 success is the textbook case of this phenomena.

These developments have resulted in a new openness in the presidential selection process. It allows an "outsider" to concentrate limited resources on early contests in Iowa, Maine, and New Hampshire with the hope of a victory which will propel the campaign into national prominence. A candidate with the time to crisscross these small states tends to gain an advantage. Under the old rules, "insiders" who held positions of responsibility in Congress or state government were considered in an optimal position to make a bid for the White House. With the media's increased focus on the early primary and caucus states, candidates who do not hold positions of responsibility are better able than those who do to spend the countless hours in these states which are necessary to build an effective campaign organization. George Bush's early success in the 1980 Iowa caucuses enabled him temporarily to pull out of the pack of Republican challengers to Ronald Reagan. Four years earlier, Jimmy Carter's victory in the same state put him permanently ahead of other contenders for the Democratic nomination. In each case, the candidate's full-time job was presidential contender. Howard Baker thought that he could use the platform of Republican leader in the United States Senate as a springboard to his party's nomination in 1980. But his failure to develop a local organization in the early caucus and primary states resulted in electoral failure and withdrawal from the race by the first week of March when only one tenth of the primaries were finished.

Critics of the system argue that this advantage for the "outsider" might open up the system but it can also produce a President who is not familiar with the day to day workings of government. A second argument raised by the opponents is that it gives a disproportionate say in the selection of the President to the voters of these small states. The presidential field is reduced by the results of these early primary and caucus elections. However, the general election tends to emphasize the industrial Midwestern states and the large Eastern states. Candidates who could do well in these areas may be eliminated from the race before they have an opportunity to compete in the geographical areas of their strength.

INFORMATION PROCESSING

The third technological revolution which affected presidential politics involves the area of information processing. Computer technology has allowed direct mail solicitation on a massive scale for both campaign contributions and electoral support. In addition, the expansion of polling and survey analysis of the attitudes and orientations of the American electorate was made possible by the computer.

These changes have resulted in an expansion of the financial base of presidential candidates. Candidates are able to go directly to a large number of Americans because of the computerized mailing technology. This advance is especially important because of the recent presidential election finance reforms. Regarding the presidential nominations process, the reforms limit any donor to a $1,000 direct contribution to a candidate with the first $250 matched by the Federal Government. A candidate, in order to qualify for matching funds, must raise $5,000 in at least 20 states from donations of no more than $250 each. The general election campaign for the major party candidates is totally financed by the federal government. These reforms heighten the need for a good direct-mail solicitation in the months before the primary and caucus elections.

The political pollster, first used as a major political adviser by the 1960 Kennedy campaign, makes the presidential candidates very sensitive to the public's wishes. But some critics argue that a candidate who consistently looks to a pollster for advice on issue positions is seeking to manipulate the public. The proponents of this practice, on the other hand, argue that a politician with a good opinion analyst will be a highly responsive officeholder, and that responsiveness is an essential element in a democratic government.

The communications and information processing revolutions have acted to replace the traditional political party organization. The party workers were at one time the candidate's link to the general public. He was dependent upon them to pass his message to the voters. Television has allowed the candidate to go directly to the public thus bypassing the party organization. The data-processing advances have also weakened the party. The candidate can go directly to the people by mail to raise money. Because of polling, he is no longer dependent upon the precinct captain to tell him what the thinking is at the grassroots level. These changes have contributed to the decay of the party organization as an effective electoral apparatus.

To summarize the impact on the presidential selection process of these three technological changes, let us look at their consequences in terms of the three standards we raised earlier: selecting the best person as President, providing that person with the broad national support necessary to govern effectively, and creating a vehicle for the discussion of national issues. On all three criteria, it must be concluded that the technological revolution has been a mixed blessing. Each advantage it brings seems to be accompanied by an offsetting problem.

Political technology has made it easier, for example, for a highly capable candidate who lacks a national reputation to overcome this disadvantage and win the presidency. On the other hand, a candidate who lacks a national reputation could just as easily be an inept amateur with a flair for using the media and other campaign technology. The new technology, therefore, can hinder as well as help the nation choose the best qualified candidate for the White House.

In terms of building broad national support, the changes aid a President by allowing him to travel across the nation as well as enabling him to reach directly into almost every living room by way of television. On the other hand, television and direct-mail campaigns can also be used to mobilize the opposition to the administration. The powerful opposition to Presidents Johnson and Nixon during the Vietnam War, for example, was due in large part to the fact that it was the first war brought directly to the American people by television. Finally, in respect to aiding the discussion of national issues, the technological changes are also a mixed blessing. They aid the debate because pollsters can give the candidates an exact idea of what issues are of concern to the American people and what programs might deal with them. Television, however, in communicating the issues, uses a short and simple format which may distort them.

CHANGES IN CAMPAIGN FINANCE RULES

In addition to the changes in the presidential selection process which have resulted from technological changes, there have also been major alterations in the laws regulating the finance of presidential contests.

The major changes in campaign finance rules have had a great impact on the nomination and election campaigns for the presidency. The 1976 election was the first governed by these changes which were intended, among other things, to encourage small contributions to presidential candidates. For 1980, an individual giving $100 or less may receive a tax credit from the Federal Government equal to half of his or her gift. Contributions of $250 or less per person are matched by the Federal Government so that the candidate would receive twice the amount of the original gift. In order to keep the federal matching funds, candidates have to receive more than 10 percent of the vote in contested primaries. Candidates failing to gain this much support in two straight efforts will lose their matching funds until they receive 20 percent of the vote in a primary. This so-called Ellen McCormick Rule was passed to prevent a nonserious single-issue candidate from filing for the matching funds and then running a purely "educational" campaign financed 50-50 by the federal treasury.

These rules have had several consequences. They tend to force candidates to enter the presidential race early, so that they can start raising the money needed to qualify for the federal aid. Secondly, they tend to discourage entries late in the primary season. Candidates who enter the fray late are at a severe disadvantage because they have to "waste" precious time in order to raise money in enough states to qualify for the matching aid.

In addition, the statutes which granted the federal matching funds also set limits on how much a candidate can raise from any donor ($1,000) or political action committee ($5,000) and how much can be spent in the preconvention phase as well as on a state-by-state basis. Candidates refusing federal matching funds, like John Connally in 1980, may spend as much as they like, but are still bound by the limits on how much any single donor or political action committee (of a business group, for example) can give them. Because few presidential candidates are willing to forfeit federal matching funds, the overall spending limits force a greater degree of national coordination on the campaigns. Ronald Reagan's 1980 campaign faced difficulties because he spent more than $12 million of the $17 million limit by early March. A candidate may use a strategy of heavy early spending in order to sew up the nomination before the later primaries are contested. Jimmy Carter's 1976 campaign is a textbook illustration of this approach. The danger of this approach is that if a candidate fails to knock out his opponents early, he will be forced by a shortage of funds to run a limited campaign in the later primary states thus curtailing his ability to reach these voters.

The reforms tend to increase the issue content of the presidential race. They aid the candidate taking positions significantly to the left or right of the center of public opinion. This is because voters who share these positions on issues are generally more highly motivated and more likely to send small contributions to candidates who espouse them. Consequently, the reforms tend to hurt candidates closer to the center on the issues because it is more difficult for them to raise the money, especially if there are two or three individuals jockeying for this position. Under the old rules, the center candidates could go to a few financial angels for the start-up money, but the campaign donation limits have forced an end to this strategy.

Thus it would seem that reforms dealing with the financing of presidential nominations and elections, like the vast changes in campaign technology, have produced mixed results. On the one hand, the reforms seem to sharpen the debate over political issues which is one desirable criterion for the presidential selection process. On the other hand, they tend to give an added advantage to candidates whose views on issues may differ significantly from the center of public opinion. Such candidates, if elected, might have greater difficulty in attracting the broad public support needed to govern effectively (which would be *contrary* to a second key criterion for a successful selection process).

Another component of the campaign finance reforms is the fact that the general election campaigns of both major parties are totally paid for by the Federal Government through the $1 check-off arrangement on the federal income tax forms. Each major party nominee gets an identical sum. This regulation tends to favor the incumbent because any challenger will need to spend more money in order to overcome the many advantages of incumbency. The rather low limits on the general election campaign expenditures also tend to increase the reliance on the electronic media for advertisements. Some critics of the system argue that these restrictions tend to reduce the more traditional use of bumperstickers, buttons, etc., and thus reduce the level of personal involvement in the campaign which in turn reduces voter turnout for the general election. Again we see that a reform designed to correct one evil (such as the excessive power of money in elections) may have unforeseen negative consequences in other areas.

The 1980 primary season produced an interesting example of the fact that, contrary to the assumptions of some reformers, money cannot buy electoral success. John Connally spent over $10 million and was able to win only one delegate to the Republican Convention by mid-March when he decided to abandon his presidential efforts. Connally's failure, despite his ability as a candidate to raise and spend money on a very large scale, illustrates the adage that a successful campaign needs to hit a responsive chord in the electorate. Money alone is not enough. If a candidate is able to do well early, money will flow in to enable him to continue to fight in the later primaries.

INCREASE IN THE NUMBER OF PRIMARY STATES

A second set of changes in the formal rules governing the presidential selection process came as a result of separate actions on the state level. The number of states using primary elections to determine their presidential choices grew from fifteen in 1968 to thirty-seven in 1980. The rules governing the selection of convention delegates are a mixture of state government regulation and state party law. The United States Supreme Court in *Cousins* v. *Wigoda,* 419 U.S. 477 (1975), held that the National Party Convention held ultimate responsiblity for determining the qualifications and eligibility of its delegates.

Each state primary has a different impact on the actual selection of convention delegates. Some are purely "beauty contests" in so far as they have no direct impact on the selection of delegates. The Vermont Republican primary, for example, requires a presidential candidate to receive over 40 percent of the vote before the results are binding on delegates. In other states, the delegates are awarded to candidates in direct proportion to the primary vote. A third procedure awards the delegates to the plurality winner in each of the state's congressional districts. A fourth variation has separate balloting for President and convention delegates. A fifth scheme has a caucus selection process for delegates with the primary results binding on the delegates for the first or second ballot for the presidential nomination.

States also differ from one another in their rules concerning who is allowed to participate in a party primary. In some states, primaries are open to all registered voters (Democrats, Republicans, Independents, etc.) who state on the day of the primary that they want to participate. In these "open" primary states, Democrats can "cross over" and vote in the Republican primary instead of their own, and vice versa. Independents may vote either in the Democratic or the Republican primary, presumably choosing the one which interests them most. In other states primaries are "closed," that is, only registered Democrats may vote in the Democratic primary and only registered Republicans in the Republican primary.

The movement toward more primaries tends to increase the impact of grassroots voters on the delegate selection process. Under the old rules, when party caucuses flourished, party leaders were able to dominate the delegate selection process, so that the people who went to the convention owed their allegiance to them. These leaders then went to the convention with the purpose of nominating a candidate who would aid them the most either in terms of electoral support in November or with future presidential patronage. Deals or arrangements were made among these leaders to build a winning coalition for a particular candidate. The proponents of the current system emphasizing primaries argue that it gives power to the people rather than to the political bosses. The critics reply that the people who participate in the primaries are not always representative of the general public. They point to the 1964 Republican (Goldwater) and 1972 Democratic (McGovern) conventions which were dominated by political "amateurs" who were more interested in their candidate's purity on the issues (close agreement with them) than in winning the election. Under these circumstances, candidates cannot hope to win their party's nomination by showing that they are more electable than their rivals. Furthermore, critics contend that emphasis on the grassroots politics of the primaries is more susceptible to the choice of a demagogue as the party nominee than was the older system in which the experienced voices of state and local party leaders were powerful enough to prevent such an outcome.

PARTY REFORMS

The political parties have also changed the rules governing the delegate selection process and convention procedures. In 1936, the Democrats repealed their two-thirds rule which had required two thirds (rather than a simple majority) of the delegates to nominate a presidential candidate. This eliminated the ability of a minority in the party to block the nomination of a candidate favored by the majority. In 1972, the Democrats outlawed the unit rule which forced entire state delegations to vote as a bloc in accord with the preference of a simple majority of the state's delegates.

The Democratic Convention in 1972 moved the party toward a "proportional" representation scheme for the allocation of convention delegates. Minority candidates who receive 15 percent or more of the vote at any stage of the delegate selection process were to be given representation at the convention in proportion to their strength. In a race with three or more candidates, this rule reduces the likelihood that any of them will achieve a first-ballot victory. The Republicans have allowed a "winner take all" system of apportioning delegates at the state or congressional district level. This rule increases the ability of the leading candidate to build a winning coalition on the first ballot at the Republican convention.

The Democrats have sought to nationalize the delegate selection process by saying that any state which does not obey the national party rules may find its delegates challenged, and perhaps rejected, by the convention. (Exceptions will be made if the state party does not control the state legislature and consequently cannot change state law governing the party process.) The Republicans have been more states-rights oriented in their approach to party rules. In other words, they are reluctant to have national party rules direct state party practices and procedures.

The reform efforts within the Democratic Party going back to the 1964 convention sought to open the delegate selection process first to blacks and then to other minorities, young people, and women. The party has consistently flirted with the establishment of required delegate quotas for representation of these various groups. The assumption has been that the party ought to redress past injustices against these groups and be sociologically representative. However, in many cases the reforms have reduced the representation of the more traditional elements of the party such as white ethnic groups and blue-collar workers.

These reforms have tended to open the presidential race to a wider variety of candidates. They have expanded the number of individuals and groups who can influence the selection of presidential candidates. Whether this has resulted in better people being nominated and elected President is an open question. Candidates now have to appeal to a wider spectrum of individuals and groups each of which judges candidates in terms of its immediate pressing interests rather than the candidate's ability to win the general election or to govern the nation effectively once elected. The reforms have not tended to benefit candidates whose positions are close to the center of public opinion. Nor have they benefited those with extensive experience in government.

Furthermore, critics have argued that party reforms have weakened the political parties themselves by weakening established party leaders, party organization, and party loyalty. In so doing, it is argued, reforms have reduced the power of the President to govern effectively. Party strength and loyalty is an invaluable tool which Presidents can use on occasion to unify a government divided into three coequal and often competing branches. Any changes that weaken the parties make the job of the President just that much harder.

Again we are confronted with the paradox of reform. Party reforms have increased public participation in the selection process *directly* by encouraging participation by a larger number of groups and *indirectly* by raising more issues and intensifying the debate over them. On the other hand, the reforms are not generally credited with creating the conditions under which more capable candidates, who can attract broad national support, can be nominated and elected. Many political observers believe that, in combination with a number of other recent political trends, party reforms have made the selection of such a President more difficult.

REFORMS IN THE ELECTION SYSTEM

The strengths and weaknesses of the electoral college system and the various alternatives to it have been analyzed in countless essays and books. What is sometimes obscured in these detailed analyses is that the debate about the electoral college system is essentially a debate over the question: *What is the best way to form a national majority in a presidential election so that it seems legitimate and binding to the people?*

Space does not permit a full discussion of all the points bearing on this question. Rather, a few salient arguments will be presented which have a fundamental bearing on the question above.

One of the most persistent criticisms of the present system is directed against its "winner take all" method of allocating electoral votes in a presidential election. The candidate who leads all others in the popular vote of a state wins *all* of that state's electoral votes. Critics argue that this distorts the popular mandate by giving nothing to the candidates who finish second, third, etc. even if they attract a large number of votes.

When the distortion is compounded by similar results in many states it can become a national distortion of the popular will. That is, the present system could produce a President who wins the election by compiling a majority of the total number of electoral votes of the fifty states and the District of Columbia, but who wins fewer popular votes on a nationwide basis than his opponent. This, in fact, happened in the presidential elections of 1876 and 1888. Such a system, critics conclude, is not a good way to form a national majority since it runs the risk of electing a "minority" President who lacks legitimacy in the eyes of the public.

Critics have proposed many alternatives to cure this and other perceived maladies of the present election system. The proposal which has clearly received the most serious consideration in recent years is the direct election plan which has been offered by Senator Birch Bayh as an amendment to the Constitution. Under the plan, there would be one direct national election. Separate state elections with their "winner take all" feature would be abolished. Every vote would count. The candidate who obtains the most votes nationwide (provided he gets a minimum of 40 percent of the vote) would become President.

Even though it had the backing of President Carter and (according to polls) most of the public, it failed in 1979 to get the two-thirds vote in the United States Senate which would have given it a favorable start. One persistent criticism of the direct election plan is that it would weaken the two-party system in the United States. Paradoxically, the very "winner take all" feature, which has brought so much criticism to the present election system, is also credited with strengthening the nation's two-party system. By eliminating it, critics contend, the direct election plan would create new problems which often accompany a multiparty system.

Under the "winner take all" method of awarding electoral votes state by state, only one candidate can win a state's electoral votes. The rest get nothing. Minor parties, faced with the prospect of no electoral reward, are induced to drop out or to align themselves with one of the two major parties. By eliminating the "winner take all" feature, the direct election plan might encourage minor parties to run national candidates. Each could chip away enough of the two major party candidates' national vote to deny either of them the 40 percent necessary to become President under the plan. With many parties in a presidential race, and no candidate able to muster 40 percent of the national vote, a national presidential election could fail to choose a leader who would seem legitimate to the American people. Paradoxically, a direct national election could produce a result which would not seem binding or legitimate in terms of majority rule.

One has only to delve this deeply into the dispute over the presidential election system to realize that it is extremely difficult to *form* a majority in a large, diverse nation, that all the methods of doing so have flaws, and that one must be willing to compromise in order to implement any attempt at forming a national majority.

A recent attempt at compromise between the present system and the direct election plan is the national bonus plan. It would keep the present system intact with one change. The change is designed to eliminate the possibility of choosing a "minority" President. Under the bonus plan, the candidate who wins the most popular votes nationwide gets a *bonus* of 102 electoral votes for doing so (2 from each of the 50 states and 2 from the District of Columbia). Under such a system, it is argued, the "winner take all" feature would continue to discourage minor parties on a state-by-state basis. However, the national bonus for the national popular vote winner would prevent this feature from contributing to the choice of a "minority" President as it did in the elections of 1876 and 1888.

Although the bonus plan appears to be a reasonable compromise to many students of politics, it could replace the present system only if a constitutional amendment was passed. It is therefore likely that the present system, which has worked reasonably well since 1888, will be retained.

CONCLUSION

Our discussion of the many facets of nominating and electing a President leads to the conclusion that the three goals set out in the beginning of the essay are not necessarily mutually achievable. A nominations system which leads to a sharp discussion of the issues may eliminate candidates who appeal to the broad and moderate center of public opinion, and who could generate widespread support once elected. A system that promotes "the best candidates" may be one which necessitates the downplaying of issues. An election system designed to give a more direct voice to the majority may increase the opportunity for minority parties to play the "spoiler" role in a presidential election.

Rules are not neutral. They tend to benefit some individuals and work against others. The determination of what rules are good and what are bad depends upon the values of the person making the decisions as well as their strategic position among the various competing interests. The one safe conclusion which can be drawn from any discussion of the presidential selection procedures is that the debate will never end, because there will always be a diversity of interests and individuals who want to change the rules in order to nominate and elect the presidential candidate most in sympathy with their views and objectives.

Suggested Readings

Herbert E. Alexander, *Financing Politics: Money, Elections and Political Reform,* Washington; Congressional Quarterly Press, 1980 (2nd edition).

Herbert E. Alexander, *Financing the 1976 Election,* Washington: Congressional Quarterly Press, 1979.

James W. Ceaser, *Presidential Selection: Theory and Development,* Princeton: Princeton University Press, 1979.

Timothy Crouse, *The Boys on the Bus,* New York: Ballantine Books, 1973.

James I. Lengle and Bryon E. Shafer, *Presidential Politics: Readings on Nominations and Elections,* New York: St. Martin's Press, 1980.

Neal R. Peirce, *The People's President: The Electoral College in American History and the Direct Vote Alternative,* New York: Simon and Schuster, 1968.

Nelson W. Polsby and Aaron Wildavsky, *Presidential Elections: Strategies of American Electoral Politics,* 5th edition, New York: Charles Scribner's Sons, 1980.

Wallace S. Sayre and Judith H. Parris, *Voting for President: The Electoral College and the American Political System,* Washington, D. C.: The Brookings Institution, 1970.

Richard A. Watson, *The Presidential Contest,* New York: John Wiley & Sons, 1980.

Stephen J. Wayne, *The Road to the White House: The Politics of Presidential Elections,* New York: St. Martin's Press, 1980.

President Nixon, Soviet Communist Party leader Leonid Brezhnev, and other United States and Soviet leaders chat informally before sitting down at the Moscow summit meeting. *(Religious News Service Photo)*

John Kennedy with people, 1962. *(The National Archives)*

Carter answers questions at a press conference. *(Karl Schumacher, The White House)*

Kennedy at a press conference, 1961. *(The National Archives)*

President Nixon gives his characteristic two-handed wave as he and Mrs. Nixon ride in the inaugural parade. *(Religious News Service Photo)*

Jimmy Carter-Gerald Ford presidential debate, 1976.

John Kennedy cabinet meeting, 1962. *(The National Archives)*

Lyndon Johnson giving pens to congressmen after signing a bill. *(The National Archives)*

Ford conferring with Secretary of State Kissinger.

Ford meeting with his cabinet.

Part II

The President and the Government

Most Americans expect their President to do a good job of "running the government." The essays in this section, however, make it abundantly clear that while a President may exert *influence* on the government, it is impossible for him to run it. Although he is often called "the head" of the executive branch consisting of almost three million civilian employees, he can only hire and fire a very small percentage of these people. The rest are hired and protected thereafter by independent personnel systems such as the Civil Service. There is a second important reason why the President cannot run, but can only influence, the numerous executive departments and agencies which comprise the bulk of the national government. He has a powerful rival for influence— the United States Congress.

Before he can make appointments to fill key positions in the various departments of the executive branch, the President must obtain the "advice and consent" of Congress's upper house, the Senate. Faced with the Senate's power to turn down his nominee, the President often finds that he must appoint someone who is not one of his top choices in order to appease a powerful senator or group of senators. Moreover, the Constitution gives the Congress, not the President, the power to appropriate the money to run the government. One of the first lessons a government bureaucrat learns is to pay as much attention (and often more) to the wishes of powerful congressmen as to those expressed by the President.

In order to have a chance even to influence a government bureaucracy of almost three million souls, the President needs help. In the postwar period he has indeed acquired many helpers. There are now several hundred workers on the President's White House staff. Even though they are supposed to be his most loyal and dependable helpers, there are simply too many of them for him to know well or to trust deeply. Hence, he draws heavily on an "inner circle" of a dozen or more trusted advisers drawn largely, but not exclusively, from this group. The President's inner circle can enhance his influence on the government if it helps him to reach out for help and support beyond the White House to key people in the bureaucracy and in Congress. On the other hand, if his inner staff reinforces any tendencies he may have to withdraw into the White House as a kind of fortress protecting him from the vast reaches of the government outside, it will only increase his sense of isolation and reduce his influence.

The President's ability to reach out and influence Congress is crucial in influencing the government because Congress passes the laws and provides the funds which direct and nurture the federal establishment. There are countless ways Congress can undercut or even undo a President who does not build a sizable amount of influence and respect among its members. One of the most important tests of a President's effectiveness in influencing the government is his ability personally, and through his White House staff, to build influence in Congress.

The description of a President bound by numerous legal and political restraints, who can command only a few people, but strives to influence just enough to lead effectively, is fairly accurate when there are no major foreign or domestic crises beseiging the nation. When such a crisis arises, however, a very constrained President may be quickly transformed into a dominant President. A crisis situation, as perceived by the President, may be as massive in scope as World War II, or as limited as President Carter's attempt in April 1980 to rescue American hostages in Iran.

The President's tendency to assert dominance over Congress in times of crisis raises some important questions. First, does he rely mainly on open persuasion to convince Congress and the people at large that his dominant role is required by the nature of events? Or does he rely mainly on secrecy and deception to mislead Congress and the public into accepting his dominance? A closely related question arises in such situations: Has the President consciously or unconsciously exaggerated the urgency of a difficult situation in order to throw off the usual political restraints and assume dominance over Congress and the rest of the government? When such questions arise in response to presidential actions, the federal courts and the Supreme Court in particular may play a key role in providing the answer. When the President stands on one side of such a question, and Congress on the other, the way in which the Supreme Court interprets the constitutional powers of each may determine the outcome.

The essays in this section point up the difficulties and the contradictions in a modern President's relationship to the government. They help the reader to understand how scholars can write about a "crippled presidency" and an "imperial presidency" and be discussing the same office.

"I'll teach YOU to remember who's boss around here !!"

1

The President and the Bureaucracy

Raymond Chambers

Bainbridge Junior College

A bureaucracy is simply a group of people who perform the routine, day-to-day activities of an organization. In American government the bureaucracy performs two broad routine functions: preparing new proposals for others to approve or reject (planning) and implementing programs approved by others.

Few people see bureaucracy favorably. In fact, the word bureaucracy has come to be a shorthand explanation for why something did not happen or, if it did, why it went wrong. Indeed, the American bureaucracy often seems to do its job poorly. It has been called wasteful, expensive, unresponsive, and uncaring. Why, for example, is it necessary to have twenty-one agencies, individuals, councils, and committees dealing with the environment, or nine groups engaged in spying, or twenty-five organizations supporting water pollution research? Sometimes the bureaucracy seems to do things exactly opposite to what should be done. Why, for example, did the Department of Agriculture permit the sale of poisoned tomatoes to consumers and why did it prohibit the sale of a safe, inexpensive milk substitute? And businessmen complain of the cost and effort needed to fill out the forms required by various agencies.

What, if anything, can be done? Many people look to the President for help. As Terence Smith put it, "the President is everyone's first resort." But, what exactly is the President's relationship to the American national bureaucracy? What could he accomplish if he wanted to?

In this chapter, attention is paid to what the popular expectations of that relationship are, the factors which should enhance presidential-bureaucratic effectiveness, obstacles to that relationship, current responses to executive-branch problems and prospects for reform. The conclusion, on balance, is that the obstacles to presidential leadership outweigh the President's resources. What the people want the President to do, then, may not be within his power.

The Constitution. What is the President's official relationship to the bureaucracy? Unfortunately, the framers of the United States Constitution seem to have written the article on the presidency as an afterthought. Article II assumes that there will be a bureaucracy, although its structure is not specified. Rather, the "executive power" is "vested in a President of the United States" who is charged with taking "care that the laws be faithfully executed." More directly, he is permitted to appoint "all other officers" of the United States. Among these may be the "principal officers in each of the executive departments" who, in turn, may be given by Congress the power to appoint "inferior officers." What these "officers" are to do, how they are to do it, and how they are to respond to the President is unclear. At most, the "principal officers may be required to give their opinions in writing" to the President on various subjects.

The Public Expectation. Perhaps a more fruitful approach to the understanding of the presidential-bureaucratic relationship would be to estimate what the public expects a President to do with the bureaucracy and then compare that expectation with what the President can and cannot do. Estimating the public expectation is not too difficult. Candidates for the presidency, after all, raise these expectations in their promises to cure the sick, feed the hungry, protect the defenseless, increase employment, and otherwise achieve all those other irresistibly desirable objectives. If elected and if Congress approves his program, the President is expected to manipulate the 2.5 million people in the bureaucracy to achieve these objectives. That is, he is expected to have *power*. He is expected to be *able* to get things done.

PRESIDENTIAL TOOLS

How is the President expected to get things done? How is he to prod several million bureaucrats into acting, especially if they are opposed to what he wants them to do? The President has several tools that presumably assist him in this task.

Appointment. One of these tools is included in the Constitution. The President is given the authority to appoint at least the "principal officers" of the departments. The authority to appoint needs to be very powerful especially if one is free to choose the personnel he wants; if unsatisfactory employees can be removed, and if the employees are in any position to do anything responsive. Unfortunately, the reality of presidential authority does not live up to any of these requirements.

In the first place, there are too many positions. The official civilian government workforce is approximately 2.5 million people. In addition, the military employs 2.6 million. "Other" employees amount to approximately one million people. And then there are one to three million people employed by 250,000 businesses and institutions as consultants under private contract, or by state and local governments working on federal programs. It is not likely that a President would personally know seven to ten million qualified candidates to fill these positions. It is also not reasonable to expect a President to know enough about these people to fire them if they were unsatisfactory.

In any event, much of this problem is taken out of the President's hands. Of the millions of employees who actually work in the bureaucracy, the President is authorized to appoint only 103,500. The remainder are hired through various independent systems such as Civil Service (now Office of Personnel Management), Foreign Service, Postal Service, etc. Most of those appointed (100,000) serve no directly useful purpose for the President (Veterans Administration Chaplains, for example). There are in fact only about 800 people who are actually hired and fired by the President, and who serve some useful purpose for him. He ought to be able to count on at least these people when he wants something done. Again, however, the expectation is not met.

Who are these 800? They fall roughly into two groups: those who work in the Executive Office and those who head the major departments or have cabinet rank for some other reason. The Executive Office, in turn, is composed of two groups: the White House staff and those who work in the Executive Office Building. Approximately 500 people work as White House staff. They tend to be people whose outstanding job in getting the

President elected is rewarded by being selected to work closely with the President. Unfortunately, these people may be great at running election campaigns but terrible at administration. In addition, they may be fiercely loyal to the President. Some or many may seek to prevent unpleasant news from reaching the President. Nixon's assistant, H.R. Haldeman, for example, "quietly gained almost complete control over whom the President saw and what the President said," according to Jack Anderson. "Nixon may consequently have been (largely) ignorant of the scandalous behavior which rocked his administration, after all." In fact, there is evidence that Nixon actually rejected some of the Watergate plans which were carried out without his knowledge.

The rest of the Executive Office consists of approximately 2,000 people most of whom are not appointed by the President. Those who are appointed, however, are acquired in the same manner as the "principal officers" (called secretaries) of the departments. The Constitution specifically requires that the President consult with the Senate *before* (advice) he decides who is to be appointed. Then, he must submit the chosen person's name to the Senate for its approval (consent). If he does not seek and listen to the advice he receives, the President may discover that his nominees are prevented from taking office. President Carter, for example, wanted to have Samuel Zagoria as one of his two nominees to fill seats on the Federal Election Commission. The Republicans (Carter is a Democrat) stopped the approval of both nominations for a year until Carter named his second nominee from a list the Republicans had provided.

The fact that the Senate has such power means that the President may nominate people he has never met and who may not even share his point of view. Such appointments are often used simply to please some powerful senator. This political payoff system should not be seen as too unfortunate, however. Cabinet appointees, for example, may not be in a position to assist the President even if they wanted to. The laws they must administer may bypass the President entirely and may direct the secretary to do the exact opposite of what the President wants. Furthermore, these appointees must rely on the cooperation of career personnel whose accumulated storehouse of information they do not share. Such a lack of information is a particularly serious problem to an appointee who may have only a vague idea as to what the department that he or she is to head actually does.

Sometimes Presidents deliberately seek ignorance in their political appointees. "Nixon considered [Secretary of State William] Rogers' unfamiliarity with the subject [foreign affairs] an asset because," writes Henry Kissinger, "it guaranteed that policy direction would remain in the White House." Kissinger goes on to stress how he and Nixon tried continually to bypass the State Department bureaucracy because of its obstructive nature.

Ignorant or not, political appointees may experience extreme difficulty in getting anything done. The Federal Bureau of Investigation (FBI) provides an interesting case in point. One director of the FBI, L. Patrick Gray, ordered the end of leaks of Watergate information to the press. "The ineffectiveness of that [order]," commented *The New Republic* "could be measured by dozens of subsequent stories from 'federal investigators,' based primarily on F.B.I. data." Gray's successor fared no better. "When I was police chief in Kansas City," Clarence Kelley admitted, "I gave an order and I knew it would be obeyed. I give an order here and I'm never sure what will happen." Neither, it turns out, is the President.

Finally, appointees approved by the Senate are frequently difficult to fire. Since the senator may have suggested the person in the first place, he or she would like to keep that person there. A President who fires a "friend" of a senator stands to lose the support he needs in Congress. The appointment "power," then, is somewhat less useful in getting bureaucratic cooperation than it appears.

Budgets. Another extremely significant tool of presidential manipulation is his control over the budgets of the executive agencies. A budget is simply a plan for spending money based on how much income is expected. By cutting the budget of an agency it is possible to stop something that had been going on (without money to do it, it can't be done) and to punish an agency for obstructing some presidential goal. By proposing an increase, an agency can be rewarded for its cooperation.

The President's budget control appears to be quite broad. He can have the Office of Management and Budget (OMB) cut an agency's budget request, for example. The Congressional Budget Control and Impoundment Act of 1974 also grants the President power to delay spending (deferrals) or cut out spending entirely (rescissions) under certain conditions.

Such apparent power is deceptive, however. Although the OMB appears to be the most cooperative agency, at least according to one study, and its personnel have "gone to bat" for the President's budget, the OMB does not have the final authority over the budget. A President who attempts to utilize the resources of the OMB's computer to impose his will on the various agencies finds very quickly that agencies have an effective end run around the President and the OMB. They simply go to Congress where the agency's clients may be the same people as the Congress's voters. There the cuts can be restored. Consider, for example, President Carter's efforts to eliminate a loan program to students in the health professions. His proposal simply "neglected" to include any personnel to administer the loans, thereby killing the whole program. Congress responded by appropriating $26 million for the loan program. Carter and Truman both tried to abolish a farm conservation program. The budget presented to Carter by Congress, however, had $190 million for the program.

In the event the congressional end run is successful, the President is then faced with the need to make the decision as to spending the money, deferring it, or rescinding it entirely. The latter two options, however, suffer two debilitating conditions. First, the law established certain categories of funds which cannot be deferred or rescinded. Second, deferrals and rescissions must be sent to Congress for review—the same Congress that approved the spending in the first place. The result appears to be, from an examination of President Carter's deferrals and rescissions published in the *Federal Register,* that most involve minor amounts in obscure agencies. On September 27, 1979, for example, President Carter deferred $61.9 million. Because of the budget year, however, the delay was only for three days, including the weekend! On October 1, 1979 he rescinded $113,673 and deferred 31 projects totalling only $1 million. The impact on the agencies and the budget was minimal at best. In short, the OMB is less than useful in helping the President "get things done."
Orders. A third tool is the President's power to issue orders (commonly called executive orders). It is this tool that probably is the cornerstone of public expectations regarding the presidency. To say the President can order an agency to do something automatically assumes that it gets done.

This assumption is unrealistic. An examination of 289 orders issued by President Nixon suggested that an average of 97 out of every 100 orders were either ignored or overruled or delayed by the seventeen agencies or departments to which they were sent.

The examples are numerous. Despite direct orders to relax pressure on southern desegregation, activity in the Office of Civil Rights continued unabated and might have increased. Twice, in 1969 and again in 1970, President Nixon ordered the destruction of a deadly poison developed for the Central Intelligence Agency. Five years later, after Nixon had left office, the toxin was still in the CIA's possession. Referring to an official in the Small Business Administration Office in San Francisco, Nixon raged, "this fellow deliberately did not—I read the memorandum—he did not carry out an order I personally gave. I wrote the order out (unintelligible). And, the s.o.b. did not do it."

One department in the bureaucracy which might be expected to be the most responsive to presidential orders is the military (Defense Department). After all, the President is not only Chief Executive, but also commander in chief. Even here, however, instances of noncooperation with the President's orders or directives abound. In 1932, veterans of World War I marched on Washington, D.C., to claim their "bonus." President Hoover ordered the army to move the marchers and their families into secure living quarters. Instead, Douglas MacArthur had his troops fire into the marchers and leisurely chase them into Virginia.

Thirty years later, President Kennedy ordered the removal of American missiles from Turkey and the end of spy flights over Russia. To avoid a possible war, the navy blockade of Cuba was to remain thirty miles offshore and Russian submarines were to be left alone. The American missiles stayed in Turkey. The spy flights over Russia continued. The navy ignored the thirty mile limit and began forcing Russian submarines to surface as well.

More recently, General John D. Lavelle deliberately violated the orders of two Presidents regarding the bombing of North Vietnam. There is some feeling that such insubordination may have contributed to prolonging the war in Vietnam. At about the same time, secret peace talks in Paris broke down and did not resume for a year.

Henry Kissinger, reflecting on his career with the State Department summed up the powerlessness of orders nicely. "The State Department," he writes, "when it receives an order of which its bureaucracy approves, is a wondrously efficient institution. When it wishes to exhaust recalcitrant supervisors, drafts of memoranda wander through its labyrinthine channels for weeks and months. But when it receives an instruction it considers wise, paperwork is suddenly completed in a matter of hours."

Reorganization. A fourth tool of presidential influence is the President's power regarding reorganizing the various agencies of the bureaucracy. He can, with certain limitations, transfer people and programs, combine or split agencies, or shift responsibilities. In this fashion he can take a project away from an agency that has been "dragging its feet" or otherwise obstructing presidential wishes and assign it to a more "friendly" group of bureaucrats.

There are a number of observations that can be made regarding these powers. One certainly involves the enormity of the task. How does one find the offending agency? As noted earlier, there are a large number of agencies with overlapping areas of responsibility. Suppose, then, that a President wanted to move a program out of one uncooperative agency into a more cooperative one. Since there are so many agencies involved in a given program, it is difficult to find out which agency is the culprit. And assuming the President and his staff had the time and interest to seriously search out the problem areas, the result might be that the villain is a department or independent regulatory agency or some other major unit that cannot be reorganized without the permission of Congress. The result of presidential effort, therefore, is likely to be confined to a futile, endless, series of reorganizations of minor units within departments.

The President and the executive bureaucracy must logically interact. The American public expects that interaction to be lopsided. That is, the President is expected to be able to direct the activities of the bureaucracy. Such direction would, after all, be democratic since the President is the only nationally elected official. He, then, is the link between the people and the units that provide services to the people. And the President has been given significant management tools: appointment of key personnel, supervision of money distribution, issuance of orders, and reorganization. In each case, though, there are weaknesses. Unfortunately, for those who would have strong presidential leadership, there are other obstacles as well.

OBSTACLES TO PRESIDENTIAL LEADERSHIP

Depending on who is counting, upwards of ten million people work in one way or another for the bureaucracy. Who these people are, what they do, why they do what they do, and how sensitive they are to the President are questions an incoming President must have answered if he is to have much success in delivering public services. It is, after all, people who make things happen or make them stop. Behavior, then, is a central problem area for presidential bureaucratic interaction.

Who are the people who work in the bureaucracy? Broadly speaking, there are four types of people involved: those nominated by the President, those selected by independent personnel boards on the basis of some objective criteria, outside experts, and those hired by nongovernmental companies hired to do the government's work.

Appointees to Independent Regulatory Agencies. Presidential appointees fill slots in all or part of four of the nine indentifiable parts of the bureaucracy: the White House office, the Executive Office, the cabinet, and commissioners of the independent regulatory agencies. It is the last group that is of interest at this point.

Independent regulatory agencies are established by Congress to control or prevent certain business practices that could seriously affect the economy. Deceptive trade practices, false advertising, discriminatory fees for hauling goods and services, sale of worthless "medicines" all fall within this category. There are approximately eighty such agencies. Their activities can have life or death consequences for people. The Food and Drug Administration, for example, prohibited the sale of a tranquilizer (Thalidomide) for pregnant women because it had not been adequately tested. Women in Europe, where the drug was available, produced horribly deformed babies, many of whom died shortly after birth. The Consumer Product Safety Commission deals with the safety of toys and publishes a list of those considered unsafe. The Federal Trade Commission required that care-labels be sewn in clothing since so many people, especially the poor, did not know how to take care of their clothes and wound up ruining them instead of cleaning them.

The commissioners who make the decisions about all these things are appointed by the President. The influence of the Senate (through its advice and consent) is felt in these appointments, of course. But, there are three other problems facing the President in dealing with these commissioners. One of them is the bipartisan requirement. With a little flexibility, the regulatory agencies are supposed to be nearly evenly balanced between Democrats and Republicans. A Democratic President, then, may be faced with having to appoint a Republican no matter who the President really prefers. Second, once these people are appointed, they cannot be removed by the President. They continue to serve until their terms, fixed by law, expire.

Finally, and perhaps most important, the prior experience of the commissioners makes it unlikely that they will respond to the popular will as articulated by the President. With significant exceptions, the commissioners tend to come from the very industries they will be expected to regulate. Admittedly, this fact means that the commissioners will have the knowledge that comes with experience. It also means, however, that established ways of thinking, friends back in the industry, and a fondness for the group that has been "so good to me," will strongly influence them. As at least one observer has noted, a President must get clearance from the industry involved before he can submit a nominee to Congress.

For example, the Federal Energy Office (eventually to become the Department of Energy) was dominated by former oil industry employees. Is it any surprise that oil prices and profits were permitted to rise while people in New England had to choose between heating their homes and eating? And again, the Interstate Commerce Commission which regulates railroads and trucking was set up because of the way the railroads were treating the small farmers who shipped agricultural products on trains. Naturally the commissioners came initially from the railroads. The sad condition of America's railroads is not surprising in view of the fact that the commissioners allowed the railroads to use their income for anything but maintaining the condition of the track, etc.

The result is that the major industries, who were the ones who were supposed to be regulated, come to be the regulators. Suppose that the President wanted to seriously crack down on a practice in the economy. There is a strong probability that he could not count on the regulatory agencies to help him out. Here is an important part of the bureaucracy, possibly affecting life, and the President can do little with it.

Merit Employees. The second type of bureaucrat is hired by independent personnel agencies, usually called "services" such as Civil Service (now OPM), Foreign Service, Postal Service, and Armed Service. These services hire the vast bulk of people in the national bureaucracy. They conduct tests to determine who might be qualified for specified jobs. Candidates are then forwarded to the appropriate personnel officers. The successful candidate serves a probationary year after which it is very difficult to remove him or her. As a matter of record, few are terminated because of the difficulty involved. In one case it took twenty-one months to fire a secretary who could not type. The job protections are specifically geared to prevent political interference from anyone, including the President. Hence, there is little reason for a career servant to cooperate with a presidential directive.

Outside Experts. The third type of person employed by the bureaucracy is the outside expert. These are most commonly found in a little known part of the bureaucracy called the advisory commission. There are 25,000 people involved in about 875 such commissions. The job of these commissions is as the name suggests: to provide expert information and advice on specified subjects. The scope of their activities is very broad. The range includes complex and important topics such as those considered by the Nuclear Waste Management Technical Advisory Group. Specialized issues are considered in such groups as the Advisory Panel on Real Estate Matters. Additionally, there is, or was, a National Board for the Promotion of Rifle Practice, a Plant Variety Protection Board, a Dance Advisory Panel, a Grazing Advisory Board, and a Board of Tea Experts.

Some of the advisory groups are composed of people appointed by the President. Others are staffed by people selected by that part of the bureaucracy creating the commission. In many respects, presidential advisory groups are largely cosmetic having little or no impact on laws or services. The President's Commission on the Causes and Prevention of Violence, for example, gathered volumes of data in a very thorough research project only to have its conclusions and recommendations ignored. The President's Commission on White House Fellowships is charged with selecting approximately seventeen people to work in the national bureaucracy for a year. The substantive impact of presidential advisory committees, then, is likely to be small or delayed.

The advisory groups for other parts of the bureaucracy are another story. Again, the consequences of their actions can affect life or death. There is, for example, an Advisory Council on Federal Reports whose job is to cut the cost of governmental studies. The council approved the idea of killing a proposal by the Department of Transportation to survey natural gas companies. The survey would have forced the companies to find their pipes and determine their condition. This information is crucial to people in construction who would prefer not to stumble across a gas pocket and get blown up. Coincidentally, between 1970 and early 1974, there were 3,559 pipeline accidents, 148 deaths, 939 injuries, and more than $8.8 million in property damage.

A possible explanation for such consequences is the membership of the advisory commissions. They tend to be dominated by, if not composed exclusively of, people from the interest that would be affected by the decisions made. After all, where else would the experts on the subject come from? So, who was on the committee recommending the rejection of the pipeline survey? Why natural gas company representatives, of course. The National Industrial Pollution Control Council was set up to advise on ways to help clean up the water and air. The sixty-three members came from the industries doing the polluting. It hardly stretches the imagination to predict that group's recommendations.

In any event, the connection of these people to the President is weak at best. How can one expect an agency to comply with a presidential request especially if "the experts" are opposed to what is requested?

Others. The last group of people working in the bureaucracy are those hired through some other mechanism than those already mentioned or who work for private companies doing government work. They work in three areas: government corporations, independent executive agencies, and private companies. In any event, these organizations operate at varying distances from the President. Independent executive agencies and government corporations are independent of presidential control. And, of course, private companies are controlled by their owners or directors.

PRESIDENTIAL RESPONSES

The preceding two sections have identified three problem areas obstructing or restraining effective presidential leadership of the bureaucracy. First is the complexity of the structure. Second is that group of factors generating an uncooperative attitude among bureaucratic personnel toward working with a President. Finally, there are the informal patterns connecting bureaucrats with interest groups and Congress which make possible the end runs around the President.

Reorganizing Structure. The size and complexity of the bureaucracy has been a point of concern for some time. In 1949, the Congress appointed a group called "The Commission on the Organization of the Executive Branch of the Government" (popularly known as the Hoover Commission). Congress specifically used the word "organization" not "reorganization" perhaps in recognition of the fact that the executive branch had *never* been organized.

More recently, President Carter made several proposals reducing the number of agencies and consolidating functions. The reduction would be accomplished by eliminating duplication through consolidation and by outright termination of agencies and groups that could not justify their existence. In nearly four years, Carter experienced mostly frustration. True, he had obtained from Congress permission to make minor reorganization assignments. He had also acquired two cabinet departments (Energy and Education). And he had announced a net reduction of approximately four hundred advisory commissions and agencies.

But these "gains" were largely illusory and illustrative of the futility of reorganization. Both spending and the number of government employees actually increased. Many of the 400 commissions in the "terminated" category were simply merged with other groups often losing neither function, people, or money, just the name. Even mergers and consolidations were not entirely successful with many education programs left out of the Department of Education and many energy agencies maintained independently of the Department of Energy.

Agency-Client-Congress Ties. The second problem is that there exists a cozy network of close ties involving agencies which serve clients who, in turn, provide campaign funds to congressmen who, naturally, come to the aid of threatened agencies. Faced with budget cuts, for example, agencies just scamper around the President and have the cut restored in Congress. Faced with extinction, agencies seek rescue in Congress. Wrote Ted Gest, what "happened to the Carter (reorganization) crusade was simply that it met stiffer opposition than anticipated from Congress and from special interests inside and outside government." Besides Congress has a natural and historical enmity toward the President. Congress sees as one of its major roles the restraint of a potentially despotic Chief Executive. What better way to prevent the abuse of executive power than by spreading it out among an array of independent and/or obscure organizations?

Reorganizing Personnel. Tampering with these conditions may not be worth the effort. Consequently, Carter turned his attention to what may well be the central problem of effective leadership of bureaucracy: entrenched behavioral reluctance to cooperate with the President. His solution to the personnel problem was essentially threefold. First, in recognition of the fact that many bureaucratic organizations overrepresent those interest groups most likely to benefit from government action, he ordered improved representation of consumers on advisory commissions and at proceedings of independent regulatory agencies. The Food and Drug Administration, for example, allocated $250,000 to help consumers pay for travel expenses to FDA hearings.

Second, on the chance that there is fraud, waste, and ignorance of management principles in the bureaucracy, he acquired a series of "inspectors general" and management improvement teams. Between rooting out the crooks, if any, and training the managers, Carter hoped for smoother service delivery by the bureaucracy.

The third Carter reform has been to split the career servants into two groups: the Senior Executive Service (SES) and the regular civil servant. Each group is to be treated differently. The SES consists of those who could be called middle management. Unlike the old Civil Service, the SES would not be guaranteed pay raises. Instead, these people would be placed on a merit system which would reward those who perform and punish or remove those who do not perform or are obstructive. The idea is to create incentive "for excellence."

Outside of this comparatively small group (about 7,500), the other civil servants would be largely immune from these rewards and punishments. They would be *hired* differently, however. The old Civil Service Commission was divided into an Office of Personnel Management (OPM) and a Merit System Protection Board (MSPB). The hiring function of OPM has been downgraded and transferred to the personnel offices of the various departments, some of whom may be in the SES and subject to incentive systems, while others may not. In this fashion, "basic management policies (can) be made by the managers themselves."

These are major steps in an area that has created many problems. But questions remain. How is "excellence" to be measured? The discussion in this chapter suggests that at least part of the measurement should include the degree of cooperation with presidential directives. But such directives could be seen as political interference, which remains forbidden in the plan. It is doubtful that cooperation with the President is what most bureaucrats and congressmen consider excellence. Moreover, SES people are still bound by laws that may conflict with presidential wishes. Indeed, the act reforming the Civil Service specifically requires each agency to set up its own standards of performance suggesting the probability of a confused pattern of cooperation or noncooperation.

Will Carter's reforms work? Over a year after the law enacting them became operational, no one had been fired. In fact, public employees had been successful in several challenges of the new rules at the MSPB. As Timothy Adams wrote, "you may have heard that it was hard to fire federal employees. Well, things have changed. Now it's impossible." Furthermore, the immunity of the lower levels of career servants from incentives reduces motivation for cooperation.

PROSPECTS FOR REFORM

The Carter program makes a significant effort at recognizing that it is people who make an organization work. But one should not expect extraordinary developments from the changes. The program simply doesn't go far enough. Lower level service delivery people remain largely unaccountable for their actions. Until Americans decide on whose shoulders public accountability should rest, the current lower level independence is not necessarily undesirable. But if one assumes that accountability should be to the public *at large* then the only representative of that public is the President. In that case, all government employees need to be made sensitive and responsive to the President.

Sunset. A number of proposals have been made to somehow "improve" the bureaucracy. Two of these, sunset and organized abandonment, do nothing to enhance presidential control of the bureaucracy. Sunset refers to a program where certain types of agencies must justify their existence before a legislature every few years. Twenty-five states have sunset laws with fifteen more considering it. The experience has been dismal. Alabama, for example, worked on 300 agencies only to terminate just one. In any event, terminating an agency does little to enhance an executive's ability to get things done. In fact, it removes a potential group from his control.

Organized Abandonment refers to a plan in which programs, not agencies, are terminated after a set number of years unless justified in writing. A variation of this plan is what Carter calls Zero-Based Budgeting in which entire programs, not just program increases, must be justified every year just to continue in force. Again, terminating a program does not mean the administrators of that program will be more responsive to the President. In fact, logically, they will be less responsive.

Personnel Changes appear to have promise. An executive needs, for example, a system that provides the information that entrenched bureaucrats may not want to provide. Technically, this process is called feedback. One method that may have merit is Franklin Roosevelt's old "Kitchen Cabinet." This group was composed of people outside of government who provided information to balance the information provided by the regular bureaucracy. Unfortunately, Carter's "inspectors general" and the management improvement teams are not designed to provide this kind of feedback but to respond to feedback provided by others.

Conclusion. The relationship between the President and the bureaucracy is lopsided in favor of the bureaucracy. Increasing presidential influence is not impossible. In a case study of welfare programs during Nixon's presidency, Ronald Randall suggested that some degree of control can be achieved on at least a piecemeal basis. And individual Presidents, Lyndon Johnson for example, have been able to secure the cooperation of selected segments of the bureaucracy by doing what the bureaucrats wanted and using negotiating skills. But what is the price in time and effort for these achievements? If increased influence is to occur (and is wanted), plans that attempt comprehensive, but gradual, changes in bureaucratic behavior may well be the only way to produce more direction and sensitivity in such an important part of American government.

Suggested Readings

The study of the presidency has been plagued by a lot of writing about anecdotes and little careful research. This situation is particularly descriptive of work in the relationship between the President and the bureaucracy. The problem is undoubtedly due to the difficulty of focusing on the subject. As the chapter noted, even the framers of the Constitution appeared uncertain as to what that relationship should be.

The student, then, is forced to dig through material that is either too narrow or too broad in scope and extract the relevant material. Among the more general sources of information is *The Presidential Studies Quarterly* (926 Fifth Ave., N.Y., NY 10021). Published by the Center for the Study of the Presidency it contains readable, scholarly articles on various aspects of the presidency. *The Washington Monthly* (1525 – 18th St., N.W., Washington, DC 20036) is a more popularly oriented periodical focusing primarily on the bureaucracy. It is more interested in the gaffs than the accomplishments, however. *The Public Administration Review* (1225 Connecticut Ave., N.W., Washington, DC 20036) provides more analytic work with occasional explicit attention to the interaction between President and bureaucracy. At the forefront of presidency research is the Presidential Studies Group of the American Political Science Association (1527 New Hampshire Ave., N.W., Washington, DC 20036).

A recent issue of *The Presidential Studies Quarterly* (Fall 1979) is devoted to the question of presidential power with some application to the bureaucracy.

A rare effort at measuring the reality of presidential-bureaucratic relationship is Raymond L. Chambers, "The Executive Power: A Preliminary Study of the Concept and of the Efficacy of Presidential Directives," *The Presidential Studies Quarterly,* (Winter 1977). More commonly, estimates of the relationship are attempted through case studies as in Ronald Randall, "Presidential Power versus Bureaucratic Intransigence: The Influence of the Nixon Administration on Welfare Policy," *American Political Science Review,* (September 1979); the reports of participant-observers such as Henry Kissinger, *The White House Years,* Little, Brown, and Co., Boston, 1979; various presidential memoirs, Dean Acheson, *Present at the Creation: My Years in the State*

Department, W.W. Norton & Company, Inc., N.Y., 1969, Joseph A. Califano, Jr., *A Presidential Nation,* W.W. Norton & Company, Inc., N.Y., 1975, and Theodore C. Sorensen, *Watchmen in the Night: Presidential Accountability After Watergate,* The MIT Press, Cambridge, Mass., 1975.

Other illuminating looks at aspects of the presidential-bureaucratic connection are: Louis Fisher, *Presidential Spending Power,* Princeton University Press, Princeton, N.J., 1975; Alan A. Altshuler, ed., *The Politics of the Federal Bureaucracy,* Dodd, Mead & Company, N.Y., 1968; and Richard P. Nathan, *The Plot That Failed: Nixon and the Administrative Presidency,* John Wiley & Sons, Inc., N.Y., 1975.

2

The President and the White House Staff

William D. Pederson and Stephen N. Williams
Yankton College, South Dakota

Although members of the White House Office do not normally receive the same degree of publicity as cabinet officers and congressmen, they sometimes exert more influence in the government than nearly anyone apart from the President himself. Indeed, on occasion key White House assistants become substitute Presidents! The most important members of the White House staff are typically drawn from the dozen or so senior political advisers to the President known today as the "inner circle," but who in the past were called "the kitchen cabinet," "the tennis cabinet," "the poker cabinet," and "the brain trust." Although membership in this exclusive circle depends on each President, it usually includes individuals such as the White House chief of staff, the assistant for national security affairs, the assistant for domestic affairs, the White House counsel, the appointments secretary, the assistant for legislative affairs, the press secretary, and the assistant for public relations, whom Garry Trudeau has more accurately dubbed "the Secretary of Symbolism."

The White House Office is a development of the modern presidency that grew out of the Second World War. In 1936, Franklin Roosevelt created the President's Committee on Administrative Management headed by Louis Brownlow, a successful city manager, to study the problem of presidential assistance. The following year the Brownlow Committee issued its report that concluded with the words "the President needs help." The Congress subsequently passed the Reorganization Act of 1939 which created the Executive Office of the President, the general managerial arm of the modern presidency.

The White House Office needs to be distinguished from the larger Executive Office of the President. The latter includes several thousand employees who are housed in two large office buildings near the White House, while the former includes several hundred employees located on the ground floor and in the basement of the White House. The "inner circle" is usually composed of the assistants who occupy the offices nearest the President's Oval Office. Its members are among the most powerful bureaucrats of the five million employees who make up the executive branch of government in the United States.

The White House Office is organized as the President wants. He appoints his staff without Senate approval. While serving him, they are not subject to congressional interrogation, and they are assigned and removed at his pleasure. Flexibility is the major structural characterization of the White House Office, particularly as shown in its expansion and organization.

Presidents have always felt quite independent in staffing the White House. George Washington took the initiative to hire an aide at his own expense after the Congress refused to provide him secretarial assistance. Subsequent Presidents continued the practice until Andrew Jackson broke the tradition by "borrowing" a bureaucrat from one of the departments to work for him in the White House at government expense. The Jacksonian precedent continues in the modern presidency as an ordinary practice. Although federal law limited the number of assistants to fourteen, for more than forty years Presidents were using hundreds of employees in the White House until the Congress finally legalized a vastly enlarged staff during the Carter administration.

In a sense, the recurrent problems associated with the modern presidency are related to the phenomenal increase in the size of the White House Office. Although the Brownlow Committee called for six presidential assistants, the number reached more than six hundred full-time employees during the Nixon administration. A White House bureaucracy has been created which stands between the President and the departments. Flexibility in its size and organization have created dangers. The "plumbers" unit, which conducted wiretaps and burglaries, was established in the Nixon White House to plug alleged national security "leaks."

Less alarming, but illustrative of the structural flexibility in the White House, was Rosalyn Carter's appointment of a chief of staff for the First Lady when her staff expanded to more than twenty persons.

Three persistent problems remain in the White House which have not been solved by the expansion of the White House staff: (1) loyalty, (2) centralization, and (3) external relations. In order to understand each of these problem areas, it is necessary to understand how the personalities involved with the White House Office interact with each other.

THE PROBLEMS OF EXCESSIVE LOYALTY: PALACE GUARD POLITICS

Although the White House Office allows for flexibility in terms of expansion and organization, there are a number of factors which push it toward rigidity and isolation. Woodrow Wilson believed the American political system, with its numerous checks and balances, cuts the President off from the support of the cabinet, the Congress, and political parties. Presidents inevitably turn toward their "inner circle" for ego support, particularly during times of crisis. As will be shown, presidential aides have a similar tendency to become dependent on their boss. The most dangerous problem of the modern presidency concerns the excessive mutual dependence that develops between Presidents and their aides. The personalities of "the inner circle" and the President become crucial in determining the degree of isolation of the Oval Office from outsiders.

The mutual dependence of Presidents and their aides is often strengthened by the "marginality" of both. Marginal persons leave their old ties behind and establish new ones to achieve greater success. They do not feel that they fully belong in their new surroundings, but cannot return to their old ones. They develop a strong need for approval and acceptance, and place great value on loyalty and conformity (James C. Davies, *Human Nature in Politics,* John Wiley, 1963).

Presidents and their aides have risen to the top of American political life. Once in Washington, however, they often feel alienated from what they perceive to be the reigning "Washington Establishment." This reaction was extremely strong with Richard Nixon and his conservative West Coast aides. But the same reaction has characterized all recent Presidents to some degree including President Carter and his Georgian staff. Thus, even Presidents and their aides may feel a lack of "belongingness" in Washington, and retreat behind a shield of excessive loyalty and conformity.

In selecting their staff, Presidents usually seek out likeminded men. Patricia Florestano has presented evidence indicating that no matter who is President, certain background characteristics are preferred in White House aides. Presidents apparently feel more comfortable with aides who are middle-age or younger, white males (96 percent), college educated (86 percent) in private schools (58 percent), and recruited from the private sector (60 percent) while working on the East Coast (77 percent).

The preferences of individual Presidents become more specific. John Kennedy liked football players and World War II veterans and Richard Nixon favored nonpracticing lawyers and military men. Six of the seven highest aides in the original Carter administration came from Georgia, so that the press tagged it "the Georgia Mafia," in the tradition of "the Missouri Gang" during the Truman administration, and "the Irish Mafia" during the Kennedy administration.

If the process of presidential selection of aides often leads to excessive conformity and loyalty, the needs of the aides themselves strongly reinforce these qualities in the form of submission to the President. The overriding need of the White House staffer is to keep his or her job. Submission, therefore, is hardly surprising in view of the fact that presidential assistants owe their jobs completely to one person. For many, their entire professional association has revolved around the career of the politician they serve in the Oval Office. Moreover, the awe of that office, if not the individual himself, encourages deference. These factors work together to produce submissive assistants who obey the President without question.

Submissiveness is often shown by an aide's attempt to make himself over in the likeness of the President. For example, William Loeb, Jr., the lower-class top aide to Theodore Roosevelt, began wearing pince-nez spectacles, a mustache and the same hair style as the President. Although reserved by nature, he adopted Roosevelt's assertiveness in the White House; although a high school drop out, he adopted Roosevelt's reading habits; and although in poor physical shape initially, he became more athletic.

He wanted to be Roosevelt! More recently, Theodore Sorenson, John Kennedy's top aide, displayed similar behavior. Although a native of Nebraska, he began speaking with a Boston accent, and adopted so many of Kennedy's gestures and other mannerisms that he was able to receive White House calls by impersonating the President.

A dilemma for White House aides is learning how to conform and be submissive, yet at the same time be noticed and promoted by the President. Too great a show of independence can lead to certain demotion. Aides, therefore, are often reduced to gimmicks or subterfuges to achieve their ends.

Gaining proximity to the President's Oval Office, for example, becomes very important. Daniel Moynihan clearly recognized this during the Nixon administration when he gave up the chance for a spacious office in the old Executive Office Building next door to the White House for a tiny office in the White House basement. Similarly, assistants realize they have fallen from grace when they lose their ground floor offices in a transfer to the basement, the fate of Midge Costanza, a public liaison assistant, before leaving the Carter White House.

Presidential assistants may also try to prove their worth by the size of their personal staffs, a factor contributing to the expansion of the modern presidency. But the primary means to prove one's loyalty is through the use of flattery and "brown-nosing." Longevity in the White House Office often seems to require nearness to the President when good news is announced and one's absence when bad news breaks. Unpleasant thoughts uttered in the proximity of some Presidents become taboo. For a President whose primary value is loyalty, this is the ideal setting to become captured by one's staff. Rather than receiving an accurate portrayal of reality, such a President encourages his own isolation by keeping aides around him who promote his imaginary view of the world.

The sort of aide who might save a President from this folly is unlikely to get into the Oval Office. Thus, what has been called the "selection-submission-subterfuge system" used to staff the modern presidency promotes excessive loyalty and isolation. With no outside references, the President becomes a prisoner of his staff. President Johnson could not understand why young people identified with Dustin Hoffman in "The Graduate." Richard Nixon could not understand "the bums" who protested against his Vietnam policy. Both Presidents turned the White House into a bunker staffed with clean-cut clones of themselves. Crisis situations further intensify the demand for loyalty among aides. Even if Presidents use outside advisers, the tendency is to ignore their advice. For example, President Nixon publicly refuted the findings of both the National Commission on Obscenity and Pornography and the National Commission on Drug Abuse.

CENTRALIZATION: A MATTER OF ORGANIZATION AND PRESIDENTIAL PERSONALITY

In every presidency, there are powerful forces encouraging submissiveness and conformity among members of the President's staff. The organizational structure of the White House, however, can either undergird these forces or act as a counterweight against them. There are two contrasting models of staff organization. The first is represented by Franklin Roosevelt's decentralized staff. It is an informal, unstructured, subordinate-centered model that tends to encourage competition, tension, and dissent in decision making. The second is Dwight Eisenhower's highly centralized model. It is structured like a pyramid. Rather than reporting directly to the President, most assistants report through a formal hierarchy to a chief of staff who then deals with the President. It is a boss-centered model that discourages open conflict.

Franklin Roosevelt acted as his own White House chief of staff. He surrounded himself with generalists rather than specialists in order to avoid dependence on a single source of information. John Kennedy's staff organization maximized the benefits of the decentralized model. Emphasis was placed on increasing the President's sources of information and obtaining opinions different from his own. Assistants received equal consideration so that a minimum of filtering of communication occurred. The main difference between the two administrations from a staffing perspective was that Roosevelt introduced greater competition among his aides than Kennedy. For example, Franklin Roosevelt once remarked, "There is something to be said for having a little conflict between agencies. A little rivalry is stimulating you know. It keeps everybody going to prove that he is a better fellow than the next man. It keeps them honest too" (Arthur M. Schlesinger, Jr., *The Age of Roosevelt,* Houghton Mifflin, 1958, p. 535). Although some viewed the Roosevelt White House as utter chaos, the system was intended to give the maximum amount of information to the President.

The greatest similarity between the Roosevelt and Kennedy administrations was the accent on equality within the White House, which is at the heart of the decentralized model. This emphasis was most clearly present in the Kennedy administration. With a person-centered orientation, John Kennedy was sensitive to those who worked for him and was able to convey his respect for them. Theodore Sorenson, Kennedy's most influential aide, recalls, "There was a rapport between the President and his staff. He was informal without being chummy, hard-driving but easy-mannered, interested in us as people without being patronizing. He treated us more as colleagues or associates than employees" (Theodore Sorenson, *Kennedy,* Harper and Row, 1965, p. 41).

Kennedy's preference for an atmosphere of equality among his advisers was reflected in his restrictions on protocol during decision making. The President learned an important lesson about the dangers of protocol early in his term. In a meeting of the National Security Council during the planning of the Bay of Pigs fiasco, Chester Bowles was prevented from voicing his strong objection to the invasion plan. At the time, Bowles was an under secretary of state filling in for the secretary of state. Protocol required silence for those "filling in" unless called on to speak. Bowles was not called upon.

After the Bay of Pigs fiasco, Kennedy decided to overcome the restrictions that protocol placed on his advisers. To encourage dialogue and dissent, he set up an office in the State Department, known as the Operations Center, where his top advisers could meet without the President and engage in dialogue as equals. This new system was tested a year later during the Cuban Missile crisis. Theodore Sorenson captures the spirit of the change:

> . . . one of the remarkable aspects of those meetings was a sense of complete equality. Protocol mattered little when the nation's life was a stake. Experience mattered little in crisis that had no precedent. . . . We were fifteen individuals on our own, representing the President and not different departments. Assistant Secretaries differed vigorously with their Secretaries. I participated much more freely than I ever had in a NSC [National Security Council] meeting; and the absence of the President encouraged everybody to speak his mind (Theodore Sorenson, *Kennedy,* Harper and Row, 1965, p. 679).

Apparently, Kennedy had sensed some of the loyalty problems of the modern presidency. He purposely was absent from some of the meetings in order to encourage dissent. Respected outsiders were invited to attend the meetings for the same reason. A robust debate followed that gave the President carefully considered alternatives for dealing with the crisis.

In addition to feeling he did not need to be the center of every discussion, Kennedy was able to tolerate the public recognition of his senior aides. For example, rather than reacting angrily to the press notice of McGeorge Bundy's important role as his national security adviser, Kennedy commented dryly, "I will continue to have some residual function." In a similar vein, during his first official trip to Paris he introduced himself as the husband of Jacqueline Kennedy, rather than as President of the United States.

In contrast to Roosevelt and Kennedy, the Eisenhower staffing system was highly centralized along elitist lines. President Eisenhower carried his military background into the Oval Office by instituting a vertical chain of command in the White House. The formality of the staffing system was suggested by the fact that his top aide was designated the first White House "chief of staff," rather than the "secretary to the President" as the post was called during the first half of the twentieth century, or the even less impressive title of "President's private secretary" as the post was called in the nineteenth century. Sherman Adams, the chief of staff during most of the Eisenhower administration, became the most powerful man next to the President. Adams handed out assignments himself, as well as deciding who and what would gain entry to the Oval Office. This suggests a built-in flaw of the centralized elitist model; its tendency to isolate the President from a variety of sources of information.

The Nixon administration carried the Eisenhower model to its logical extreme, and in the process revealed its major limitations and inherent dangers. H. R. Haldeman, Nixon's chief of staff, also controlled everybody and everything that went into the Oval Office. If a staff member attempted to circumvent the system, or go beyond his specific role, he was severely reprimanded. For example, Jeb Magruder found this out after he proposed a new idea in a memo and forwarded it to Haldeman for the President to read. The chief of staff immediately stopped the memo in his office, and quickly returned it with the abrupt comment,

"Your job is to do, not to think" (Lewis Paper, *The Promise and the Performance,* Crown: 1975, p. 120).

The strong emphasis placed on order and division of labor in the elitist organization hinders dialogue. If reports and memos were to have any chance of gaining the attention of President Eisenhower, they had to be no longer than one page. Similarly, if ideas were to have any chance of penetrating the Oval Office during the Nixon administration, they had to be put on paper. President Nixon disliked dialogue and refused to engage in the give and take that is characteristic between a President and his aides in a decentralized system.

A formal chain of command and protocol discourages conflict in a staffing system. Yet a President's personality can be just as oppressive as these structural devices for maintaining order. For example, Lyndon Johnson's staffing system illustrates its kinship with the centralized-elitist model. Rather than relying on a permanent chief of staff, he used his domineering personality to exert control over the smallest matters during his administration; rather than letting his staff have some access to the media, he alone dealt with the press; and rather than establishing rapport with his assistants he kept them continually off guard, thereby creating "an atmosphere of permanent intimidation" (Doris Kearns, *Lyndon Johnson and the American Dream,* Harper and Row, 1976, pp. 238-242).

A former presidential assistant during these years aptly captures the master-serf relationship that Johnson's personality established in the White House:

> The President would berate his aides in lashing language. Sometimes he did this collectively, as when he exploded at three of them in his office, "How can you be so goddamn stupid! Why can't I get men with the brains of the Kennedy bunch?" More often, he would turn on a single staff member. On a number of occasions I saw an aide emerge from a presidential session white-faced and shaking, swearing that he could not stand it another day. (Eric F. Goldman, *The Tragedy of Lyndon Johnson,* Knopf, 1969, pp. 120-121)

Johnson used his intimidating personality to stifle dissent. He had an obsession for making decisions by consensus in his dominating presence. As in the Nixon administration, those who challenged policies during the Johnson administration were let go or lost access to the President. Such Presidents view others as objects rather than as equals. Both administrations erred in an attempt not just to maintain order, but to assert absolute control over subordinates.

The ever-expanding size of bureaucracy and the desire of Presidents to govern their administrations has led the modern presidency in the direction of centralization. Although there seems to be a near ritual requiring new Presidents to voice a desire to return to a decentralized staffing model, most recent Presidents have inevitably discovered the need for hierarchy. For example, both Gerald Ford and Jimmy Carter stressed at the outset of their administrations that they intended to have decentralized staff systems to avoid the pitfalls of the Nixon administration. Both discovered that a great deal of confusion and chaos resulted from their attempts at decentralization. Finally, both moved to centralize their staff organizations, but not to the same degree as had Presidents Eisenhower and Nixon.

It is probable that if Franklin Roosevelt were faced with the huge executive bureaucracy of today, he would be forced to adopt a more centralized system than he used in the 1930s. The lesson of the Ford and Carter presidencies would seem to be that time and efficiency require some hierarchy in a large bureaucracy, such as the modern presidency. The problem is to have enough order to avoid chaos, without so much order as to turn aides into obedient serfs.

There is some evidence that psychologically healthy Presidents are best able to achieve the balance between centralized and decentralized staff systems that is needed in providing leadership for the modern presidency. James David Barber has classified Franklin Roosevelt, Harry Truman, John Kennedy, Gerald Ford, and Jimmy Carter, as the healthiest Presidents of the modern presidency, based largely on their high degree of self-esteem and flexibility, in contrast to the lower self-esteem and greater inflexibility of Dwight Eisenhower, Lyndon Johnson, and Richard Nixon. There is also evidence to suggest that the elitist staff systems required by Presidents with relatively low self-esteem contribute to low morale among White House staffers. The highest turnover rate among the staffs of recent Presidents occurred in the Johnson and Nixon administrations, suggesting greater employee dissatisfaction working under an elitist system. The only two dismissals of chiefs of staff because of scandals (Sherman

Adams and H. R. Haldeman), also occurred in elitist staff systems. Moreover, the President and the two chiefs of staff who subjected their aides to the worst personal abuse (Lyndon Johnson, Sherman Adams, Eisenhower's chief of staff, and H. R. Haldeman), operated similar systems.

On the other hand, our healthiest Presidents seem better able to attract the most gifted aides, for example, the cases of Franklin Roosevelt and Harry Hopkins, John Kennedy and Theodore Sorenson, and Gerald Ford and Richard Cheney. Surely the most important aide of the entire postwar presidency, in terms of positive contributions to a number of Presidents, has been Clark Clifford, who began as special counsel to Harry Truman. The Truman-Clifford association, based on equality and mutual respect, represents a model of the type of relationship that is possible in a relatively decentralized staffing system.

It is difficult, at the conclusion of one four-year term, to state with certainty whether Jimmy Carter's White House staff conforms more closely to a highly centralized, or to a less centralized pattern of staff organization.

Carter initially vowed to avoid a hierarchical, highly centralized system. Yet James Fallows, chief White House speechwriter during President Carter's first two years in office, complained that the White House staff was, first and foremost, an entrenched hierarchy. He observed that everyone in Carter's White House had a fixed place "from God and the angels, through kings, noblemen, and serfs, down to animals, plants, and stones. . . ."

Fallows also observed among Carter's White House staffers the low morale often found in highly centralized staff systems. He agreed with journalist Jeff Greenfield's characterization of the Carter team as "the President's Sad Young Men." (Fallows, *Atlantic Monthly,* June 1979, pp. 76, 79.)

Although James David Barber has classified Jimmy Carter as a modern President possessing high self-esteem in marked contrast to others such as Johnson and Nixon, there has been a great deal of skepticism about this assessment of Carter. Professor Fred I. Greenstein, for example, spoke for many political observers when he stated that beneath Carter's great composure "is a personal lack of confidence in being able to do the job." *(National Journal,* July 28, 1979, p. 1239). James Fallows similarly observed in Jimmy Carter an "insecurity at the core of his mind and soul." (*Atlantic Monthly,* May 1979, p. 46.) There is no doubt that Carter sincerely wanted at the outset of his presidency to avoid the pitfalls of excessive hierarchy and centralization in his White House staff organization. But it may well be that he lacked the high self-esteem necessary, not only to live with, but to effectively manage the conflicts and discomforts which are a natural product of less centralized and less hierarchical staff systems.

EXTERNAL RELATIONS:
BUILDING BRIDGES OR BARRICADES?

The "insiders" within the White House Office who are closest to the President's Oval Office have experienced a variety of problems with those outside of it during the modern presidency. In fact, these problems have spread from the traditional critics of administrations, such as members of the Congress and the media, to those within "the President's branch of government," particularly in the executive departments. Presidential assistants in the White House "inner circle" have increasingly come to view themselves as an extension of the President's personality whose proper role is to guard him and his policies from outsiders who might have priorities different from those of the President. As a result, mutual tensions are generated between insiders and outsiders that may develop into a rivalry or even a hostile relationship.

There are structural factors in the modern presidency that contribute to these difficulties. The expansion of the White House Office from a staff of forty-five during Franklin Roosevelt's administration to an impersonal bureaucracy of more than five hundred full-time employees during recent administrations, inevitably fuels suspicions between the insiders and outsiders. White House staffers tend to be young amateurs devoted to the success of a single individual in the Oval Office, in contrast to the older, more established professionals in the cabinet and the Congress who are dependent on a variety of sources for their success. Furthermore, the insiders tend to think and work within a relatively short time frame of four to eight years, while the outsiders are more likely to have a much different perspective since they are likely to be in Washington longer than one or two presidential terms.

A bureaucracy inside the White House encourages the President to challenge and perhaps even dominate the views of outsiders much more readily than in the past. This adds to the suspicions of those who have lost in the power shift as policymaking has moved from the departments to the White House during the modern presidency. For example, relations between the State Department and the White House ebbed during the Nixon administration when he turned his national security adviser, Henry Kissinger, into the de facto secretary of state who made American foreign policy. Secretary of State William Rogers was often kept in the dark regarding policy changes until after Kissinger had made the decisions. Foreign service officers in the State Department became flunkies in the policymaking process.

This departure from the traditional role of the State Department in the formulation of foreign policy spread further suspicions to the Congress which had no power to confirm, and lost its power to question the new White House policymakers. President Nixon refused to permit any of his insiders to testify before the Congress. This was the first time a President established an absolute prohibition against testifying under the guise of executive privilege, a customary practice used by Presidents to withhold information from the Congress regarding activities within the executive branch of government. Congress clearly was threatened with losing much of its investigatory power under Nixon's policy.

Presidents have the choice to increase or decrease the suspicions that have developed in the modern presidency by the tone they set for their administrations. Generally, the personalities of Presidents seem to influence the degree to which they are willing to build bridges to outsiders or construct barricades around the White House. As policymaking has moved into the White House, healthy Presidents are most likely to recognize the need for personal negotiation and compromise with outsiders, as well as the necessity of tension and conflict in democratic politics.

The political styles of Richard Nixon and John Kennedy, particularly in their dealings with cabinet officers, suggest the difference between psychologically healthy and unhealthy Presidents. A clear pattern of closure emerged during the Nixon administration. For example, he began his administration with a 1968 television extravaganza promoting the virtues of each of his cabinet members, but four years later ended up collectively emasculating them during a mandatory mass resignation ritual. A suspicious President wanted to purge those whom he saw as disloyal department heads. Nixon's treatment of his cabinet officers is also suggested by his lack of personal contacts with the majority of them. For example, Walter J. Hickel, secretary of the interior, complained in 1970 that he had seen the President only twice during his sixteen months in office. Rather than personally negotiating with outsiders, Nixon spent more than sixty percent of his time alone with H. R. Haldeman, his chief of staff (John Kessel, *The Domestic Presidency*, Duxbury, 1975, p. 114).

In contrast to Nixon's penchant to control outsiders from behind "the Berlin Wall" around the White House, Kennedy continually looked outside the government for advice and was sensitive to the needs of the departments and other outsiders. Indeed, he tried to make outsiders feel like insiders. For example, although he appointed a powerful national security adviser in the White House, he also involved his secretary of state in policy development. Kennedy allowed greater independence for his cabinet officers who were allowed to run their departments on their own. He allowed his secretary of defense to fill all the important positions in the Pentagon with his own men. Rather than relying on a chief of staff to shield him from cabinet members, Kennedy acted as his own chief of staff and allowed a high degree of personal access to cabinet members. The differences in the Nixon and Kennedy treatment of cabinet members are indicative of how they generally handled other outsiders, such as members of the Congress and the news media.

At the outset of his presidency, Jimmy Carter veered sharply from the Kennedy pattern toward the Nixon pattern of dealing with his cabinet. During his first months in office, he seemed determined that his cabinet members be treated like true insiders and have the power of insiders. He vowed that during his presidency, there would never be an instance where members of his White House staff would dominate or act superior to the members of his cabinet.

By the spring of 1978, however, President Carter had clearly become less trustful of the loyalty of his cabinet members. He therefore shifted the balance of power away from them toward the trusted members of his White House staff.

Then in July of 1979, the most dramatic and sudden shift

of power occurred. Carter asked for the resignations of all his cabinet members and accepted almost half of them. The inner group of White House staffers, sometimes called "the Georgia mafia," emerged untouched and dominant after the great cabinet shakeup.

Carter's sudden and massive move against his cabinet was more reminiscent of Nixon's approach to "outsiders" in his administration than Kennedy's. *Newsweek* magazine noted that the danger in the sudden "purge" of cabinet members was that it might produce "a garrison mood" in the Carter White House in which "dissent is perceived as disloyalty and the whisper of the [White House] courtiers is mistaken for the voice of America." (*Newsweek*, July 30, 1979, p. 28.)

Fundamentally, a President sets the mood for his administration in its dealings with outsiders. Because healthy Presidents have flexible personalities, their personal relationships with insiders and outsiders are likely to promote understanding. Robert Kennedy's account of the Cuban missile crisis captures an essential characteristic of his brother's personality:

> The final lesson of the Cuban missile crisis is the importance of placing ourselves in the other country's shoes. During the crisis, President Kennedy spent more time trying to determine the effect of a particular course of action on Khrushchev or the Russians than on any other phase of what he was doing. What guided all his deliberations was an effort not to disgrace Khrushchev, not to humiliate the Soviet Union, not to have them feel they would have to escalate their response because their national security or national interests so committed them. (Robert Kennedy, *Thirteen Days*, Norton, 1968, p. 102).

Flexible personalities tend to have the empathetic skills that are necessary for democratic politics. Kennedy's ability to empathize, even with his opponents abroad during a crisis, sharply contrasts with Nixon's treatment of his opponents at home: "One day we will get them—we'll get them on the ground where we want them. And we'll stick our heels in, step on them hard and twist. . . get them on the floor and step on them, crush them, show no mercy." (Charles Colson, *Born Again*, Chosen Books, 1976, p. 72.) The mood that Richard Nixon set for his administration is eerily reminiscent of George Orwell's *1984*, "If you want a picture of the future, imagine a boot stamping on a human face—forever."

SOME TENTATIVE CONCLUSIONS

The three main problems of the modern presidency in relation to staffing are linked to the phenomenal growth in the White House Office. The loyalty problem arises out of the tendency of individuals to associate with persons like themselves. The pressures of the White House reinforce this tendency to such an extent that Presidents may end up talking to themselves. A possible solution to the loyalty problem is to use a decentralized staffing system, yet there seems to be an inevitable need for hierarchy in large organizations. The trend toward centralization is complicated by the fact that Presidents use the type of staff system that best fits their personalities. Unfortunately, the least healthy personalities select systems that further isolate them from political reality. Finally, the problem of establishing and maintaining successful relationships with outsiders has become more difficult as policymaking has been moved into the White House bureaucracy, but once again, it seems that the personality of the President and his empathetic skills strongly influence the relationships that are likely to emerge.

Suggested Readings

The standard works on White House staffing include Patrick Anderson, *The President's Men* (Garden City, New York: Doubleday, 1968); Richard T. Johnson, *Managing the White House* (New York: Harper and Row, 1974); and Stephen Hess, *Organizing the Presidency* (Washington, D.C.: Brookings Institution, 1976.) A fascinating new work is Michael Medved, *The Shadow Presidents* (New York: Times Books, 1979). Two books which thoughtfully examine the pressures toward submission and conformity in the White House environment are George Reedy, *The Twilight of the Presidency* (New York: World, 1970) and Irving Janis, *Victims of Groupthink* (Boston: Houghton Mifflin, 1972).

The best study of the psychological aspects of presidential performance is James David Barber, *The Presidential Character,* 2nd ed. (Englewood Cliffs, N.J.: Prentice-Hall, 1977). The first empirical test of Barber's theory is William D. Pederson, "Amnesty and Presidential Behavior," *Presidential Studies Quarterly,* Vol. 7, No. 4 (Fall 1977), pp. 175-183. The modern classic that relates psychology to politics is James C. Davies, *Human Nature in Politics* (New York: John Wiley, 1963).

An article that puts White House staffing in a comparative politics perspective is Russell Baker and Charles Peters, "The Prince and His Courtiers," *Washington Monthly,* Vol. 4 (February 1973), pp. 30-39. Two important empirical studies are Michael G. Fullington, "Presidential Staff Relations," *Presidential Studies Quarterly,* Vol. 7, Nos. 2-3 (Spring-Summer 1977), pp. 108-114; and Patricia S. Florestano, "The Characteristics of White House Staff Appointees," *Presidential Studies Quarterly,* Vol. 7, No. 4 (Fall 1977), pp. 184-191. Recent works on staffing in the Carter administration are James Fallows, "The Passionless Presidency," *Atlantic* (May and June 1979), pp. 33-48, 75-81; and Bruce Adams and Kathryn Kavanagh-Baran, *Promise and Performance* (Lexington, Massachusetts: Lexington Books, 1979). Excellent articles concerning relations between Carter's White House staff and his cabinet have appeared in the *National Journal.* (See November 18, 1978, p. 1852; July 28, 1979, p. 1236; August 18, 1979, p. 1356.)

Carter talking to House Speaker "Tip" O'Neill and Senate Democratic leader Robert Byrd. *(Karl Schumacher, The White House)*

3

The President and Congress: The Domestic Tangle

Frank Kessler

Missouri Western State College

The shock of Watergate and the frustrations of Vietnam seem to be fading from our national consciousness as America enters the 1980s. Still, the sins of past Presidents are destined to be visited on their successors. The deceitfulness of the Johnson and Nixon administrations and the ineffectiveness of the numerous domestic experiments of the New Frontier and the Great Society have left Congress leery of presidential leadership. While Congress is likely to rally around beleagured Presidents in foreign policy crises, the last decade demonstrates that Congress has no intention of following the White House lead in domestic affairs simply because the President asks. Legislators evidently believe, as John Kennedy once put it, that "domestic politics can only defeat us but foreign policy can kill us." (Wildavsky, *Perspectives,* 1975, p. 450)

A number of factors have complicated the already strained relationship that the Constitution encourages with its system of checks and balances. In this chapter we shall examine some of these difficulties and the obstacles they represent to a President's initiatives in domestic affairs.

During the 1970s, Congress staked a number of claims for itself in economic policymaking. Using the Budget and Impoundment Control legislation of 1974, Congress developed its own budget system to parallel the President's. In addition, each house created a budget committee. To assist in these new fiscal undertakings, the House and Senate created a special Congressional

Budget Office (CBO) to improve legislative information and analysis of departmental budgets. Presidential impoundments* were curtailed by a provision that permits either house to block them by a simple resolution which the President may not veto. Future Presidents may not imitate Richard Nixon's efforts in 1972 to destroy an agency like the Office of Economic Opportunity (OEO) by simply withholding funds from it. To weaken other programs he didn't like, Nixon either cut funds or delayed spending on legislation related to food stamps, mass transit, low rent public housing, and a number of the domestic innovations which were carryovers from the Johnson administration. Today, the President's argument that he was justified in impounding due to the inflationary nature of the programs would no longer be sufficient. Congress would have to agree. Nixon's contempt for Congress and the response to that attitude on Capitol Hill weakened presidential leadership in domestic affairs. To many in Congress, legislative restrictions on presidential power seemed imperative because the White House was not to be trusted.

HONEST, DECENT PRESIDENTS AREN'T ENOUGH

When Richard Nixon informed the public that he was not a crook, the credibility of the presidency as an institution had hit rock bottom. The office was in dire need of an image change. The next two Presidents more nearly fit the church-going, God-fearing, personable, clean as a hound's tooth image that could stand in stark contrast to the negative perceptions that Vietnam and Watergate had generated. Jimmy Carter parlayed his "outsider image" and hard work at the grass roots into the Democratic nomination and later election in 1976. His standard sermonette about making the government as decent and honest as its people did not have the same positive effect on Congress as it had on the public. It became evident, as one Carter aide later noted with dismay, that "it's. . .a habit with Congress to oppose the administration." Optimists thought that a Democrat in the White House would get along well with the Democrats on the Hill, but Carter's honeymoon with Congress, like those of his two predecessors was

---

*White House orders to the Treasury Dept. to withhold funds already appropriated by Congress.

short-lived indeed. Even the staff members who worked for congressmen were predisposed to question White House initiatives because 2,000 of them had never served while a Democrat was President. They were accustomed to an adversary relationship with the White House.

Public perceptions of Jimmy Carter's high moral character never wavered; but would-be Presidents like Edward Kennedy questioned Carter's performance and ability to lead in light of his failure to enact comprehensive national health insurance or energy programs. Candidates like Kennedy and John Connally of Texas seemed to be saying that "nice guys" don't necessarily make the best leaders.

Until the crisis in Iran, precipitated by the taking of American hostages, Carter's performance rating was the worst recorded in the history of major polls on presidential performance. That rating, though, could well have said more about public expectations of the presidency than about the job one President, Jimmy Carter, was doing. Professor Richard Neustadt suggests that Americans expect entirely too much of their Presidents. (Neustadt, *Presidential Power,* 1976, pp. 69-76) The public evidently doesn't understand that, as Prof. Thomas Cronin suggests, "only rarely can the President succeed in bringing about large scale social change." (Cronin, p. 239)

Campaigners and their promises are partly to blame for the rising expectations among American voters. In a Washington *Post* article, for example, ninety-five of the Carter promises were evaluated after his first year in office. Congress passed only half of those he presented as legislation (twenty-one of forty-three) and totally rejected four. Legislators turned thumbs down to major Carter efforts to get public financing for congressional races. Strong lobby pressure doomed White House efforts to end federal funding for all abortions, and defeated administration attempts to repeal the federal ban on common situs picketing by labor unions. Interest groups whose favorite programs did not survive the legislative maze commonly held the President accountable and faulted his leadership.

Why can't honest, decent Presidents get things done in Congress, especially when, like Jimmy Carter, they devote a great deal of effort to the task? A large part of the answer lies in problems which are beyond the President's control.

BARRIERS TO PRESIDENTIAL INFLUENCE

Presidents in the 1980s will have to deal with many of the same social problems which occupied Presidents Kennedy and Johnson, and a host of new ones as well. The economic realities of the coming decade, though, will severely restrict the options for future Presidents. They will not be able to adopt a Lyndon Johnson "war on poverty" philosophy which says that when social problems need tending, cost is not a major obstacle. In the summer of 1965 LBJ gave his Special Assistant Joseph Califano the following list of legislative goals for the coming year.

> There are three areas of urgent concern for the 1966 legislative program. The transportation system of the country is a mess. I want to do something about it. Second, we must show the people of this nation that the cities can be rebuilt. I want a program to totally rebuild the ghettos of this nation. We need an open housing bill. School desegregation and equal employment are not enough. (Califano, p. 47)

Johnson-type, Great Society programs would have a slim chance of passage in today's Congress, not because the problems they attack are unimportant; but because they would be considered budget busters in America's double-digit inflation-plagued economy. Congressmen no doubt realize that the voters will hold them accountable if government gets too big and spends too much. In response to a 1978 Gallup Poll on "Important Economic Problems/Spending and the Budget" 76 percent of the sample felt that government was spending too much while a mere 15 percent saw spending as about right or too little. In the same survey, the sample responded to the question, "What is the most important problem facing the country today?" Sixty percent answered inflation in living costs whereas only 14 percent saw unemployment as their major concern.

Traditionally, economists have suggested that the bitter pill needed to cure inflation is economic slowdown. Tightening the money supply and raising interest rates usually cool down business expansion. To those who lose their jobs in the wake of such White House and Federal Reserve decisions the cure is worse than the disease. Unemployment invariably hits hardest in the Northern urban areas. As the United States population shifts to the Sun Belt of the South, voter concerns for the social problems of the Northern cities will most likely take a back seat to their worries about the buying power of their own dollars. Future administrations will be forced to take these sentiments into account and scale down their expectations even though labor and civil-rights interest groups will fault them for not doing enough for minorities, the unemployed, and the cities. Inflation, which weighs so heavily in the domestic equation for the United States in the 1980s, is, to an extent, an internationally spawned problem beyond the control of either the President or Congress.

"Intermestic" Complications. America's economic well-being is becoming increasingly dependent upon Third World sources of oil and other raw materials. As a result, presidential conduct of *international* relations tends to have substantial *domestic* impact. Professor Bayless Manning calls this the "intermestic" problem. (Manning, p. 307) Plans to aid the Israelis in the 1973 Middle East war, for example, spawned the Arab oil embargo and the round of drastic oil price increases which have been major catalysts in producing double-digit inflation. Presidential decisions to seek self-sufficiency in energy by cutting consumption of foreign-produced oil and calls for new American autos to be more energy efficient have helped dry up the domestic large car market and drive Chrysler into desperate financial straits.

Presidents find themselves at odds with Congress too, when voters are demanding relief from inflation and, at the same time, interest groups are pressuring Congress to approve inflationary legislation to protect American products from foreign competition in United States markets. As cattle prices plummeted in 1977, ranchers pressed President Carter to reimpose quotas to limit import of cheaper Argentine and Australian beef. The administration had originally lifted those restrictions to ease grocery costs for consumers. Likewise, a presidential decision to cut back United States grain sales to certain countries as a weapon to deal with high OPEC prices can have a domestic impact on farmers. They have come to depend on overseas markets for capital to keep ahead of the rising costs of implements, fertilizers, and fuel for their farm machinery. Congressmen from agricultural states can be expected to vote for their constituency in these matters just as oil-state lobbyists will surely encourage members of the House and Senate to fight attempts to reimpose regulations on oil prices and windfall taxes on oil company profits. A frustrated Jimmy Carter told a convention of MFA farmers in Columbia, Missouri, in the summer of 1978 that it is difficult to develop national policies when the public attitude tends to be "every man for himself."

Who Initiates Domestic Legislation? Though the founding fathers were careful to separate the lawmaking and executive powers, the President has become a major legislative initiator. Congress expects the White House to provide the major themes and legislative packages for each session. The public and legislators have become accustomed to a White House shopping list, or as Richard Neustadt put it:

> a handy and official guide to the wants of its [Congress's] biggest customer; an advance formulation of the main issues in each session; a workload ready to hand to every legislative committee. (Neustadt, "Legislation," p. 104)

It would be inaccurate to suppose, though, that Congress merely sits back and waits for the President to present his formal goals and individual pieces of legislation. Committees, and increasingly even subcommittees, propose new laws in response to the requests of interest groups and in reaction to information gained through lengthy investigation. Often these proposals act as counterpoints to the approaches that the President is expected to take to the same problem.

Certain situations encourage congressional leadership in domestic affairs even though the general rule is presidential direction. Among the situations which spur Congress to preempt presidential initiative have been cases:

a) when the President is a Republican and the Congress Democratic (or vice versa).

b) when the President doesn't seem to care about something that Congress is interested in.

c) when a President is so tied down with foreign affairs that he lets domestic matters slide.

d) when interest groups encourage some action to help them or stave off some White House-proposed legislation that might hurt them.

e) when the issues involved are basically of a "pork barrel" nature. . . *ie.,* public works, urban renewal, small business loans, education grants, and so on.

and finally

f) when issues of labor relations and jobs are involved as was the case in the Taft-Hartley Law (1947), the Landrum

Griffin Act (1954), and more recently the Humphrey-Hawkins (1976), "full employment" legislation. (Pious, pp. 147-173) In each of the cases above, deferring to the President can have a harmful effect on the legislator's chances of being reelected, and so they encourage initiatives by Congress.

Reforms on Capitol Hill: New Problems for the President. During the last half-decade or so, the ancient rules of the game in Congress have undergone extensive changes. Many of these reforms have made the passage of White House programs more difficult. Throughout the 1970s, both parties have moved to democratize the committee structures of Congress. The freshman class of 1975 on the Hill seemed bent on changing the lowly status normally assigned to newcomers. They had no intention of being the pledges of the legislative fraternities, and they sought an immediate piece of the action including appointment to the prestigious committees like Ways and Means in the House and Foreign Relations in the Senate. With the spreading of power in the House, aggressive and creative lawmakers can rise to the top more quickly than in the past. A case in point would be Representative Richard A. Gephardt (D-MO) who was interviewed in the *National Journal.* In the past, second-termers were viewed as hardly dry behind the ears, yet this St. Louis legislator led the charge against President Carter's pet hospital cost containment legislation. As the young Democrat explained, it wasn't easy but he did what he felt must be done.

> Well, it wasn't a very happy experience because I am a supporter of the President and have. . .tried to be helpful and supportive. . . .But, from the outset, I was in disagreement on the hospital cost containment bill. (*National Journal,* December 15, 1979, p. 2108)

Gephardt's comments suggest that younger members of Congress like to consider themselves both loyalist and independent. Above all, they are not reluctant to use their new powers.

By 1979, over one half of the House membership had served only since Watergate. Rank and file Democratic members now vote, due to rule changes, in the party caucus to select the chairmen of Congress's powerful standing committees. As a result of these changes, at the beginning of the 94th Congress, some venerable House committee chairmen fell victim to reform. They either retired or were defeated for reelection to chairmanship of

Banking (Wright Pattman), Ways and Means (Wilbur Mills) and House Administration (Wayne Hays). As regular newspaper readers no doubt realize, the personal hijinks of the latter two had something to do with their precipitous fall from power. The removal of these aging autocrats put committee chairmen and other senior members seeking chairmanships on notice that job security was no longer assured on the basis of one's seniority as it had been in the past.

These reforms proved to be a mixed blessing for Presidents. On the bright side, many of the former conservative Southern chairmen who stood in the way of civil rights and other social reforms moved to the sidelines. Liberal congressional Democrats had come a long way from 1969 when they were forced by the seniority system to deal with Senate committee leadership which included Louisianians chairing Agriculture and Finance, a Georgian running Appropriations, Mississippians chairing Armed Services and Judiciary, to name a few. In the House, such crucial committees as Ways and Means and Rules had Southern conservatives in the driver's seat.

Subcommittee reforms between 1970 and 1975 also weakened the stranglehold that conservative committee chairmen could use on liberal White House programs. By 1974, rules changes in the House replaced domination by committee chairmen with subcommittee power. The new rules forced chairmen to share authority with their subcommittee members in many of the important areas of committee and subcommittee action.

Strengthening the subcommittees at the expense of the committee chairmen did cause problems for the President along with the advantages we have discussed. Though committee barons were autocratic, they did provide a network that an administration could use to line up votes. In the past, a President could rest assured that his program would be given favorable floor action if he could sell it to the appropriate standing committee chairman and the majority leadership. Today, increasing subcommittee autonomy and the fears of committee chairmen, who must now stand for reelection, have forced Presidents to turn their attention more and more to the rank and file members.

The reform spirit reinvigorated the old practice of taking policy positions in the House Democratic party caucus. During the Nixon-Ford years, the caucus debated the Vietnam policy, set a party-line on Watergate, sought a war powers act and created a new budget process. Nor was the Democratic caucus reluctant to challenge a Democratic President. In 1979, it rejected Jimmy Carter's original oil deregulation plans by a better than two-to-one vote.

CHANNELS OF PRESIDENTIAL INFLUENCE

While the barriers to presidential influences with the Congress are considerable, there are also channels through which the President can increase his influence with the legislative branch. The President's skill in using these channels can in large measure determine the success of his administration.

Being loyal to the President may often be the last thing on the mind of many of today's congressional Democrats. A liberal Democrat may sit in the White House, but a conservative coalition of Republicans and conservative Democrats may have great strength in Congress. As we indicated earlier, the nation is thinking conservative and is eager to tighten the belt on federal spending. For these reasons, if Presidents expect to pass domestic social legislation, the cooperation and assistance of the top Democratic leaders in Congress (the speaker of the House and the Senate majority leader) are essential. Party reforms in the 1970s increased the institutional powers for both Speaker Thomas P. (Tip) O'Neill and Majority Leader Robert Byrd. Their powers permit them to manipulate certain facets of the legislative process.

The powers granted to the speaker and majority leader also help them develop black books full of IOUs that they can call in to support a President who is able to work effectively with them. While it clearly helps the President to do so, cultivating the friendship and cooperation of the majority party leader in the House and Senate will not ensure that they either can or will convince independent-minded Democrats on Capitol Hill to follow the President's program.

Not every President has the political sixth sense about Congress that Lyndon Johnson displayed. Jimmy Carter, for example, had great difficulty learning the legislative ropes. Less than one week after he took the oath of office, he ruffled the feathers of Senate Majority Leader Robert Byrd by beginning action on his own legislative program without consulting the party leadership. Carter's initial choice for CIA director, Theodore Sorenson, became the first high level nominee for an executive position to be rejected by Congress since 1925. Prior consultation with the Senate leadership beforehand would have demonstrated that the nomination would be in trouble due to Sorenson's distaste for covert CIA activities. The novice President's major aide for congressional relations, Frank Moore, and close personal aides like Hamilton Jordan found it difficult to imagine that they couldn't handle the House and Senate in the same "ham-fisted" manner that had been effective with the part-time Georgia legislature. As one Democratic senator put it in a conversation with Elizabeth Drew,

> They came in with contempt for Congress, thinking they could bulldoze and stare it down. Then, they got subjected to a series of rebuffs, and, not having the experience to deal with it, became overly impressed with it. (Drew, 1978, p. 78)

Senate Majority Leader Byrd was not the only leader in Congress to be piqued by the amateurs around the new President. House Speaker Tip O'Neill was reportedly incensed at Carter's first two appointments from O'Neill's home state of Massachusetts. The President appointed two REPUBLICANS, Elliot Richardson to head the United States delegation to the Law of the Sea Conference and Evan S. Dobelle as protocol chief at the United States Department of State. Hamilton Jordan, Carter's special assistant in the White House, had not even consulted O'Neill. During the summer of 1978, the speaker was infuriated again, this time because the President had dismissed an O'Neill crony from the scandal-riddled General Services Administration (GSA). The speaker responded by barring Carter's emissary to Congress, Frank Moore, from his office. To help mend fences, though, during the cabinet reshuffling of the summer of 1979, the name of Representative/Lt. Governor Thomas P. O'Neill, Jr. surfaced as a forerunner for the job of secretary of transportation. That tidbit of news obviously did not go unnoticed by his father, the speaker.

Despite all of the White House *faux pas,* O'Neill was a party trooper, and he stood by the President and made every effort to push the White House energy package through a balky Congress. He repudiated his colleagues for their "lack of guts" for refusing standby gas rationing power for the President because they feared constituent backlash. Nevertheless, O'Neill continued to hold some resentments against the Georgia "good ole boys" at the White House, especially Hamilton Jordan. The speaker reportedly often referred to the President's chief of staff as "Hannibal Jerkin." Mending fences with the speaker could be done more easily since he was a seasoned party veteran, but keeping up with the rank and file House member proved more difficult.

Communication and Rewards: White House Liaisons with the Hill. A President willing to spend his days with nothing but personal contacts with congressmen would find maintaining regular contacts with 535 legislators virtually impossible. To bridge the inevitable communications gap, Presidents have used liaisons to do their day-to-day bidding on Capitol Hill. Dwight D. Eisenhower was the first President to establish a modern liaison operation with responsibility centered in the White House. John Kennedy and Lyndon Johnson tightened up the operations even further by ordering that all departmental and agency liaisons must coordinate their efforts with the White House operation. Lawrence O'Brien, top liaison officer under both Kennedy and Johnson, had regular access to both Presidents. That access gave him clout on the Hill. Like his predecessor under Eisenhower, he provided information about White House plans and helped to line up votes in both houses. His system departed from the Eisenhower mold in that O'Brien's operatives were not ashamed to dangle patronage to help get things done.

Nixon's operation was headed by former Eisenhower liaison chief Bryce Harlow. The President held Congress in such low esteem that he did little to upgrade the operation beyond adding more assistants, and diluted Harlow's clout by not meeting regularly with him. The fact that Nixon intended to dismantle many of the Great Society programs did little to endear him to Democrats on the Hill.

Interim-President Gerald Ford, drawing on his experiences on Capitol Hill, tried to revive the operations which had fallen into such disarray in the final days of the Nixon administration. Ford met daily with his liaison chief, Max Fridersdorf, and other top assistants to hammer out priorities for that day in Congress. When Ford's legislative strategy called for governing by veto (he issued sixty-six) Fridersdorf was assigned the thankless task of lining up the votes necessary to sustain the President's vetoes. (Congressional Quarterly, *Electing Congress*, p. 68-71)

The early months of the Carter administration's liaison operation under Frank Moore have variously been described as "a comedy of errors," "a fiasco," and an "unmitigated disaster." Moore evidently bruised a number of legislative egos by neglecting to return phone calls, missing appointments with legislators, and neglecting to consult with the Democratic Party leadership. After this shaky start and a number of mid-course corrections, the liaison operation improved under the watchful eye of Vice-President and former Minnesota Senator Walter Mondale.

One of the major explanations for the improvement was the fact that the administration lowered its goals on the number of bills it expected to get Congress to pass. In an insightful article on domestic policy and congressional complications, Elizabeth Drew quoted Speaker O'Neill about the administration's tendency to consider every piece of domestic legislation as "priority." On December 16, 1977, O'Neill reportedly suggested:

> . . .we had too many balls in the air. . .we have to consider our own political angle. If he sends something up here about the environment, there's a certain segment that will be watching to see if we pass it. It could be mining legislation or water diversion, it could be health. And people up here can't act on ALL OF THESE THINGS. (Drew, 1978, p. 76)

The Carter operatives had a lot to learn.

If Carter expected to sell his energy, health insurance, reorganization of civil service, and other major programs, he had to learn how to concentrate his efforts more effectively. The White House adopted an innovation they called a "task force" which paid handsome dividends in Carter's efforts to scuttle the B-1 bomber and sell the unpopular Panama Canal Treaties. The operation was intended to see that no tools of presidential persuasion were left rusty from disuse. White House lobbyists were responsible for identifying the undecided members to be brought in to speak with chief White House aides, state and defense officers, or the President himself. Carter used this system to uphold his veto of an extensive public works bill and to engineer reforms of the civil service promotion system. The outsider was learning to use the tools of persuasion at his disposal.

Pampering Congress: The Tools of Persuasion. There are three broad categories of favors that Presidents can dangle before members of Congress to get their attention: a) project monies, b) appointments, and c) courtesies and campaign aid.

PROJECT DOLLARS

The most popular pieces of domestic legislation on the Hill tend to be those which ladle out federal funds for projects like post offices, courthouses, jails, parks, highways, waterways, and so on. Once, for example, an HEW secretary was offering solid evidence for cuts in some impacted aid monies (to areas with federal installations). When he finished his testimony, the subcommittee chairman reportedly asked, "Mr. Secretary, I have one question. How much money does my state get under that program?" When the secretary said $185,000, the senator shot back, "How can you expect me to vote against a program which puts $185,000 into my state?" (Drew, 1978, p. 66)

It should come as no real surprise that large defense installations were built in the Southeastern states during the time when Southern chairmen were set like concrete in the key positions. Could it be, for example, that the White House decision to place the manned spacecraft center in Houston had anything to do with the fact that the House Appropriations Committee chairman was George Mahon, Ways and Means was chaired by Wilbur Mills, a neighbor from Arkansas, and the Banking and Currency Committee was the personal preserve of another Texan, Wright Pattman? It is indeed a curious coincidence that the architect of the 1958 Space Act (Califano, p. 59-60) was Senate Majority Leader Lyndon Johnson and that his interest in space was shared by a fellow legislator from the Lone Star state, House Speaker Sam Rayburn.

Until late into his second year in office Carter was loathe to spoon out project grants as political gravy in trade for votes on the Hill. One of the White House aides put it this way:

> The president does not believe in project grants. If the president found out that there was a member of the White House who traded a dam for a vote, that would certainly be the last trade that would be made. Besides, those projects are getting more controversial back at home. (Davis, 1979, p. 293)

Nevertheless, there are those who suggest that a number of votes on the Panama Canal treaties were purchased with resurrected public works projects, or as one political wag put it, "I hope the Panamanians get as much out of those treaties as some senators."

APPOINTMENTS

A second, and only slightly less sweet plum at the President's disposal to get votes on the Hill is the patronage job. The various civil service acts have trimmed back on the spoils system; but the White House still has a number of rewards to grant to the faithful on the Hill. The President and his department secretaries control about 6,700 positions including: 3,500 top executive department jobs, 140 White House employees, well over 500 federal judgeships, 93 United States attorneys, 94 United States marshalls, and 2,100 positions on boards and commissions. Politics has been described as "who gets what, when, and how." (Ripley, 1978, p. 300) Dwight Eisenhower complained that he had little time to do anything in his early weeks in the White House but to take job requests from Republicans who wanted to cash in their twenty years of service as loyal party workers. Initially, Jimmy Carter committed himself to making judicial appointments without political considerations. He made no such promise about United States attorneys and became embroiled in controversy when he removed Republican James Marston from his job as United States attorney in Philadelphia. It turned out that Marston was hot on the trail of misdeeds by two Democratic congressmen, one of whom, Joshua Eilberg, pointed out to the President that the position should be held by a Democrat. By 1979, at least one candidate for a seat on the federal bench, Archibald Cox, found himself being passed over probably because of his long-standing friendship with Senator Edward Kennedy. A commission appointed by the President to suggest nominees for the federal court positions had placed Cox at the top of its list for a Circuit Court appointment.

The bargaining power of future Presidents will be affected by the fact that the stocks of patronage jobs are shrinking. Eric Davis, in an interview with a few of the Carter liaison officials, found them frustrated with the dearth of jobs that could be tapped for political leverage on the Hill.

> With patronage, there have been a lot of problems. First of all, there's simply a lot less patronage to go around. . . . The plum book put out for John Kennedy in 1961 was a

couple of inches thick. The plum book we had was maybe 1/5 the size...What they (the Ford administration) did was to take a political job, abolish it, and create a new civil service job. The job description had all the proper civil service words in it, and it said nothing about being involved in political work. (Davis, 1979, p. 293)

The comments above demonstrate that the Ford administration had severely restricted the White House pool of jobs to distribute. In the city of Chicago, for example, there were 80,000 federal jobs but, according to one Carter aide, the White House could only appoint five persons.

Even when Presidents do have jobs to broker with, they must be sure to make them available to senators who still cherish "senatorial courtesy." Senators are in an excellent position to play havoc with White House appointments to the federal bench or any executive position because the Constitution gives the Senate the power to exercise consent over these appointments. President John Kennedy, for example, ran into difficulties with the Senate over his plan to nominate NAACP counsel and later Supreme Court justice, Thurgood Marshall, to a federal judgeship on the Second United States Court of Appeals. James O. Eastland, a Mississippian, and long-time chairman of the Senate Judiciary Committee, kept holding up the nomination from committee action (which he could not do under today's rules). Later, Eastland met with the President's brother, Attorney General Robert Kennedy, and suggested, "Tell your brother that if he will give me Harold Cox, I will give him the nigger" (a disparaging reference to Marshall who is black). Cox, a classmate of Eastland's college days, was appointed to a federal judgeship of his own. Kennedy knew that there were senatorial strings attached to his power of appointment.

COURTESIES

Because the number of appointed federal jobs has been shrinking, Presidents have to resort to smaller favors, little amenities, and sharing the prestige of the White House with congressmen and senators. They may invite legislators to picture-taking sessions at the White House or for special functions or gala dinners. The more personal these get-togethers, the more effective they may become. Lyndon Johnson's barbeques, especially at the

Texas ranch, were legendary. (Kearns, 1976, pp. 222-32) Along with the food and festivity came a heavy dose of effective arm twisting. Presidents can also take to the campaign trail to help congressmen and senators. If the President is demonstrably popular, his visit can be a major plus for fellow party members seeking reelection. On the other hand, if a President is not terribly popular, his appearance can be the kiss of death. At a Colorado stop in 1978, for example, Jimmy Carter referred to Democratic Senator Floyd Haskell as a national treasure. On election night, Colorado voters, who weren't enchanted with Carter or with Haskell's liberal voting record and his support of the Panama Canal treaties, buried their "national treasure" under an electoral landslide. In general, though, the visit of Air Force One on the campaign trail is good for a few IOUs for the President when controversial issues come up later in Congress.

CONCLUSION

Prospects for major White House initiatives against chronic domestic problems are slim in the foreseeable future. Inflation, energy costs, and public demands for smaller government will limit both the White House reach in these areas and the congressional willingness to cooperate with an increased federal role in attacking the social problems of the nation. Congressional reforms will make it even harder for Presidents to build the necessary coalitions to sell new domestic packages in Congress. The "every man for himself" philosophy that President Carter bemoaned, and the increasing effectiveness of interest groups in American politics, make consensus building even more unlikely. Activist Presidents seem doomed to frustration as they are forced to pander to the prejudices of individual members, subcommittees, and groups in Congress. James Fallows, a former White House speech writer and idea man, resigned due to his disillusionment with the status quo in presidential-congressional relations. "It's time to go," he complained, "when your imagination is limited to ideas that are possible to get through Congress." (Sherill, 1979, p. 119)

The only salvation for Presidents who seek to initiate needed domestic programs is to make every effort to build coalitions that cross party lines on controversial issues and use the limited plums available to the White House to develop goodwill on the Hill.

Suggested Readings

Dodd, Lawrence C. and Bruce I. Oppenheimer (eds.) *Congress Reconsidered,* New York, Praeger, 1977. This book of readings draws on top names in the field including: Charles Jones, Richard Fenno, and James Sundquist, to name a few. Discusses the newly resurgent Congress and is especially useful in parts III and IV on congressional reorganization and its impact.

Cronin, Thomas, *The State of the Presidency* (2nd. ed.) Boston, Little-Brown, 1980. Excellent insights from a former White House Fellow and congressional aide. While this is a generalized treatment of the presidency as a whole, its congressional relations section (ch. 6, pp. 187-222) provides as lucid and up-to-date a handling of the topic as is available including prominently such issues as: emergency powers, executive privilege, impoundments, and legislative vetoes.

Edwards, George C. III, *Presidential Influence in Congress,* San Francisco, Freeman, 1980. A treasure trove of vignettes and case studies which asks why there is so much conflict between the President and Congress, it also addresses in a spritely manner such questions as: how does presidential prestige and popularity affect dealings with Congress, and what legislative skills are needed to influence Congress.

Fisher, Louis, *The President and Congress,* New York, Free Press, 1972. Already considered a classic in the field written by a Congressional Research Service financial expert. Its approach is both historical and public-law oriented and examines the pre-Watergate seeds of conflicts between the branches with notable care for research.

Hughes, Emmett John, *The Living Presidency,* New York, Coward, McCann and Geoghegan, 1973. Excellent account of the evolution of presidential power and its uses up to Nixon. Written from the insider perspective of a former Eisenhower White House aide.

Livingston, William, Lawrence C. Dodd and Richard L. Schott (eds.), *The Presidency and Congress: A Shifting Balance of Power?* Austin, Texas, Lyndon B. Johnson School of Public Affairs, 1979. Discusses individually the evolution of the relationship in the 1950s, 1960s, and 1970s. The articles are part of a symposium on the subject which seems to suggest that the balance has not shifted as far to Congress as some might think.

Mansfield, Harvey (ed.) *Congress Against the President,* New York, F.A. Praeger, 1976. Covers most of the conflicts between the branches in the 1960s and 1970s with special emphasis on budgetary conflicts being useful. Also good are the sections on changing congressional staffing systems. Based on the Annals of the American Academy of Political Science, 1975. Argues for more power to Congress.

Sorenson, Theodore, *Watchmen in the Night,* Cambridge, MIT Press, 1975. Close Kennedy aide (JFK) argues the need for other political institutions such as Congress and the courts to make the President more accountable. Clearly presented format rich with insights from the inside.

Other References Cited

Joseph A. Califano, *Presidential Nation,* New York, W. W. Norton, 1975.

Congressional Quarterly, *Electing Congress,* Washington, D.C., Congressional Quarterly Service, 1978.

Thomas Cronin, *The State of the Presidency,* Boston, Little Brown, 1975.

Eric Davis, "Carter's Legislative Liaison," *Political Science Quarterly,* Summer, 1979, p. 293.

Elizabeth Drew, "Engagement with the Special Interest State," *New Yorker,* February 27, 1978, p. 78.

Louis Fisher, *The Constitution Between Friends,* New York, St. Martin's, 1978.

Bayless Manning, "The Congress-The Executive and Intermestic Affairs: Three Proposals," *Foreign Affairs,* January 1977, p. 307.

Richard Neustadt, *Presidential Power: The Politics of Leadership,* New York, Wiley, 1976.

————————, "The Presidency and Legislation: Planning the President's Program," *American Political Science Review,* December, 1955, p. 1014.

Lawrence O'Brien, *No Final Victories,* New York, Doubleday, 1974.

Kevin Phillips, *The Emerging Republican Majority,* New Rochelle, N.Y., Arlington House, 1969.

Richard Pious, *The American Presidency*, New York, Basic Books, 1979.

G. Russell Pipe, "Congressional Liaisons: The Executive Branch Consolidates Its Relations with Congress," *Public Administration Review,* March 1966.

Randall Ripley, "Carter and Congress" in Steven Shull and Lance Leloup (eds.), *The Presidency*, Brunswick Ohio, Kings Court Press, 1979, pp. 68-70.

Allen Schick, "The Budget Bureau that Was: Thoughts on the Rise and Decline and Future of a Presidential Agency" in Aaron Wildavsky (ed.) *Perspectives on the Presidency*, Boston, Little-Brown, 1975.

Robert Sherill, *Why They Call It Politics*, New York, Harcourt-Brace, 1979.

Lyndon Johnson signing the historic Gulf of Tonkin Resolution on Vietnam. *(The National Archives)*

4

The President and Congress: Foreign Policy

John M. Lewis
Indiana University at South Bend

Every President eventually discovers, if he does not already know it when he enters the White House, that the central preoccupation of his days in office must be his relationship with Congress. He can meet few of the expectations and responsibilities of his job unless he can win a substantial and continuing measure of congressional support. Yet he lacks the means of readily ensuring that support, and must therefore devote much of his energy, time, and skill to building and nourishing it. If he fails in this, he will fail in most of his other enterprises.

The framers of the Constitution expected a good deal of conflict to occur between the President and Congress. The ambition of one branch would be checked and balanced by the ambition of the other. This constitutional gulf at the heart of the national government has set the characteristic style of American national government for nearly two hundred years. And while its effect has been most marked in domestic politics, it has also frequently had a decisive impact upon the nation's foreign policy. In foreign affairs as in domestic affairs, the President has usually had to find a way to get along with Congress or face disappointment and defeat.

From the beginning, relations with foreign governments were thought to be primarily the responsibility of the Chief Executive. Even Thomas Jefferson, a very strong opponent of executive power, stated in 1790 that the "transaction of business with foreign nations is Executive altogether." When foreign affairs involve military considerations, as they often do, then the President's constitutional position as commander in chief strengthens his position further. Indeed, the most expansive claims of presidential authority, made, for example, by Lincoln, Franklin Roosevelt, and Nixon, have been based upon the commander-in-chief clause. Yet even here the President must turn to Congress for things he cannot provide for himself.

For the conduct of foreign affairs the President needs, above all, two commodities that only Congress can provide. These are, first, legal authority, and secondly, money. Without legal authority he will not for long be listened to by those he must try to persuade. Without money he cannot raise and maintain the essential tools for his job—advisers, soldiers, weapons. A third commodity a President will eventually need if he is to be successful is the confidence of his fellow citizens that he is proceeding wisely in the conduct of their affairs. While congressional support is not absolutely essential to earn public confidence, its absence for any prolonged period inevitably erodes that confidence. For though the public may revile Congress as factious or corrupt, they usually demand that the President pay it at least a decent respect and earn its occasional approval.

Different Presidents and Congresses have evolved their own different ways of doing business together; and these have changed according to the varying impact of public expectations, of personal styles and skills of Presidents and congressmen, and of America's changing position in the world. Yet, in spite of this variety, two broadly different patterns stand out. There are occasions when a President attempts to control the conduct of foreign affairs himself and to allow almost no participation by Congress. On the other hand, there are times when the President clearly acknowledges a major role for Congress, and expends great effort to win its support.

These two patterns, of dominance and partnership, should not be thought of as two quite different, distinct kinds of policy-making. Rather, they are tendencies and matters of emphasis. Much of the time, presidential conduct of foreign policy shows aspects of both. But the differences are real nonetheless, and it is useful to analyze in some detail the characteristic features of each pattern.

PATTERNS OF PRESIDENTIAL DOMINANCE

Presidents occasionally attempt to dominate policymaking in foreign affairs, to rely upon the powers and authority of their office in achieving their goals, and to ignore or exclude Congress in the process. The President and his subordinates in the executive branch formulate, authorize, and implement policy. Congress is reduced to the passive role of onlooker or, at best, to reacting to the President's actions after the event.

Presidents are most likely to adopt this high-handed approach when the nation's security seems threatened by military attack or when American military forces are committed to action. At these times, Congress and the nation turn to the President as commander in chief; they expect and accept his vigorous leadership. A crisis involving military action calls for swift, decisive, and often secret decision making. These are resources the President possesses and Congress does not. Besides, the Constitution gives the President the supreme command of the military, a mandate very few Presidents have been willing to share with Congress.

For this pattern of dominance to succeed, then, there must be a general expectation that circumstances require it. Sometimes the reality of imminent military danger is so apparent that the President has no difficulty asserting his dominance. More commonly the danger is less obvious, and the President must persuade Congress and the public to allow him exceptional authority. Even if he succeeds in this at the outset, he may have difficulty in maintaining his dominance if the crisis is protracted or if his policies do not appear to be meeting it. Thus dominance is seldom easily won and never easily sustained. Usually a President must depend upon skillful use of his persuasive resources. If the crisis is prolonged, the President will encounter increasing impatience among congressmen who resent giving up their share of decision making. It is unlikely that even the most popular and persuasive President can completely neutralize this impatience. But he must at least contain and limit it if he is to keep for himself the dominant position.

Some Presidents have tried to assert their dominance by misleading Congress and the public. Either they have misrepresented the real nature of the crisis in the belief that only in that way can an ignorant nation be aroused to action; or they have tried to conceal their policies for fear that the nation would repudiate them if they were known. And sometimes Presidents have done both. Such stratagems may work for a while: a President has innumerable ways to control information to some extent. But in the long run, doubts arise and the President's dominance—and his policy—are in danger of precipitous collapse. In that case, Congress may strike back by placing new legal restrictions upon the President's freedom of action.

Any President who tries to dominate policymaking is likely to face a congressional reaction eventually. He will probably be content, however, if he can delay that reaction until the crisis is past and the need for dominance is no longer pressing.

A number of brief case studies will illustrate and further explain these points.

First, the way in which President Lincoln mobilized the Northern states in the Civil War is the outstanding example of successful presidential dominance. While not strictly an example of foreign affairs, Lincoln's policy concerned the Union's military security and involved action against an enemy behaving like a foreign nation.

Within a few months of his inauguration in March 1861, Lincoln had not only taken actions without legal or constitutional authority: he had taken actions clearly prohibited by the Constitution. For example, he vastly expanded the size of the state militias and of the regular army and navy; he appropriated funds from the Treasury for these and other needs; he instituted a naval blockade against Southern ports; and he suspended the writ of habeas corpus in places particularly vulnerable to Confederate sabotage. For all these actions the Constitution explicitly or implicitly requires congressional authorization. But Congress was not in session at the time. Lincoln waited many weeks before calling them into session—and then told them what he had done and asked for their approval. Later in the war he repeatedly took similar unilateral actions, informing Congress only after the event.

Congress generally approved. It often did so grudgingly, belatedly, and protesting that its members should have shared in the decisions. Indeed, Lincoln's conduct provoked frequent hostility in Congress. But he never allowed it to reach such a pitch that it might seriously hamper his freedom of action.

Lincoln used several devices to maintain congressional acquiescence in his dominant position. First, in order to win the support of individuals or groups in Congress, he sometimes allowed political considerations to influence his choice of commanders—and even his choice of tactics and strategy. Many of his senior generals, and his supporters in Congress, bitterly criticized him for this. But he knew that the support of Congress and of the nation was as vital to victory as was the success of the armies. Secondly, he occasionally—though rarely—permitted his critics in Congress some small triumph over him, as when he accepted their arrest and imprisonment of a general who had displeased them. But generally he denied Congress any right to interfere in what he insisted were his prerogatives as President and commander in chief.

Most important of all, Lincoln used his own gifts for rhetoric to arouse national and congressional support. Public sentiment supported, indeed demanded, war in 1861. But it took the President's very considerable persuasive skills through speeches, messages to Congress, letters, and interviews to sustain that support through four long years of often imperceptible military progress. His critics in Congress tried to turn the 1864 presidential election into a plebiscite on his war and reconstruction policies. His victory in the election, and his opponent's defeat, underlined his continuing ascendancy.

In summary, Lincoln maintained his dominance in the conduct of the war by squeezing every drop of authority out of his role as commander in chief, by making concessions to congressional opinion on unessentials, by his use of rhetoric to justify his actions, and by the ultimate success of his policies. After the war, the congressional reaction set it. But Lincoln was no longer there to reap the whirlwind.

A more recent example of successful presidential dominance was President Franklin Roosevelt's preparation of the nation for war in the years before Pearl Harbor. During his first term as President he had largely ignored foreign affairs. But by the late 1930s he saw that the United States would have to be awakened from its isolationist slumber in order to confront the burgeoning militarism of Germany, Italy, and Japan. Once the European war began in September 1939, he concluded that the United States would probably be drawn in eventually, and that the best policy meanwhile was to give all possible aid to Britain and France.

Throughout the 1930s, however, Congress had enacted a series of neutrality acts designed to keep the United States out of foreign wars. These laws, and the continued neutralist sentiment in the country, seriously limited what Roosevelt could do to prepare.

He adopted a three-fold strategy. First he allowed events to sharpen public and congressional awareness of the danger. German conquests in Europe and successes in the Battle of the Atlantic all served to undercut the isolationist mood. Secondly, he used public speeches, radio broadcasts, and press conferences to lead public opinion, underlining the lessons of events and drawing his countrymen's eyes toward the darkening future—yet cautiously not moving so far ahead of public opinion that he provoked widespread isolationist suspicions.

Thirdly, Roosevelt undertook unilateral actions, sometimes concealed from public and Congress, designed to dramatize the trend of events, to nudge them along, and to prepare for the future. It was here that he asserted his dominance over policy, relying upon his authority as President and commander in chief to safeguard the nation's security. For example, he authorized secret planning sessions between the American and British military staffs; he gave fifty elderly destroyers to the British in exchange for military bases in the Western hemisphere; he ordered the navy to undertake patrol and convoy duty in the Atlantic Ocean where he knew American ships would inevitably be drawn into combat with German submarines; and he ordered the transfer of military supplies to the hard-pressed British at a time when American forces were themselves dangerously under-equipped. All this was done on his own authority. Congress was informed, if at all, only after he had made his decisions.

However, in contrast to Lincoln, Roosevelt was limited in what he could do and say because he knew he could not move too far ahead of a skeptical public opinion—not even clandestinely. While acting unilaterally in some areas, in others he sought congressional approval. For example, in September 1939, he called Congress into special session to repeal the embargo provisions of the Neutrality Act—in order, he said, to keep the United States out of the war by helping Britain and France to win it themselves. He showed his mastery of congressional politics by giving his lieutenants in the Senate and the House of Representatives a free hand to make deals and concessions as they thought necessary. As a result, Congress repealed the embargo. The President later declared an "unlimited national emergency," and was then able to draw upon a great reservoir of authority granted by Congress over several decades of earlier legislation. In the spring of 1941, he asked Congress to grant him vast and largely unspecified authority in the Lend-Lease Act, authority to transfer American munitions to Britain, to China, and later to Russia. Congress did so.

Roosevelt's dominance, between 1939 and the end of 1941, was thus less stark than Lincoln's had been in the Civil War. Yet he did occasionally act alone, committing the nation to momentous policies. But he also worked with Congress, to the extent that he could persuade them to sanction his policies. His success ultimately rested upon his ability to carry public opinion with him—not fast enough, perhaps, for the interventionists; too fast for the isolationists; but at a rate that had already brought the country to the brink of war with Germany when Japan attacked Pearl Harbor. The 1940 election campaign gave his opponents the chance to accuse him of pushing the country into war. His reelection, like Lincoln's in 1864, revealed the extent to which he had retained public support.

Roosevelt and Lincoln followed the same pattern in many respects. The main ingredients of the pattern were their reliance upon their unilateral authority as commanders in chief and upon their assertion of presidential prerogative; their constant and skillful leadership of public opinion; and their successful limitation of congressional hostility by occasional well-timed concessions. Roosevelt's task was in some ways harder than Lincoln's: his military crisis was more remote and less obvious. He therefore moved less far and more slowly. But like Lincoln, he retained congressional acquiescence for as long as he needed it. He too provoked an eventual congressional reaction against presidential dominance—but, again like Lincoln, he was not there to suffer it.

Examples drawn from the period of the Vietnam War show that a President's attempt to dominate military and foreign policy may be unsuccessful, leading to the collapse of his policies and to his own humiliation. Both Lyndon Johnson and Richard Nixon sought dominance: the former in the escalation of American involvement in the war, and the latter during American withdrawal and the "Vietnamization" of the military effort. Each President tried to ignore Congress on some issues and to mislead them—and public opinion—on others. Each tried to lead and mold public opinion, and each largely failed. Nixon, in particular, suffered a congressional reaction while still in office.

In 1964 and 1965, Johnson decided to commit American ground forces to Vietnam, in addition to the military advisers and bomber forces already there. He did this in spite of promising, in the 1964 presidential election campaign, to leave the fighting to the Vietnamese. In the next four years American forces in Vietnam grew to half a million.

These actions were taken, however, with some measure of public and congressional backing. In August 1964, after a naval incident off the coast of North Vietnam, Congress passed the Gulf of Tonkin Resolution. This expressed Congress' support for "all necessary measures to repel any armed attack against the forces of the United States and to prevent further aggression." Not only was this a very broad grant of support; it was also, in Johnson's view, merely a welcome endorsement of what the President already had authority to do on his own as commander in chief. And it was founded upon serious deception by the administration: the incident in the Gulf of Tonkin was, at the very least, grossly exaggerated by the President. Furthermore, he did nothing to correct Senator Fulbright when during the Resolution debate the senator assured some hesitant colleagues that "there is nothing in the resolution, as I read it, that contemplates" sending United States troops to Vietnam. He added that "that is the last thing we would want to do."

Throughout his presidency, Johnson continued to exclude Congress from the real decisions about Vietnam, except when he sought legislative authorization for more money and men. At first, Congress and the public supported him, believing his claim that the nation's security was threatened. But dissent grew as the war escalated with no end in sight. In Congress, Senator Fulbright, chairman of the Senate Foreign Relations Committee, and Senator Mansfield, the Democratic floor leader, led the opposition to the President. Johnson responded by asserting his prerogatives and by condemning his adversaries as "nervous nellies" and friends of the North Vietnamese enemy. Lacking both the arguments and the rhetorical skill to rally support for his policies, he continued them in a thickening atmosphere of secrecy.

However, opposition in Congress was still fragmentary: Johnson still received the money and men he wanted. His decision in 1968 to reverse the policy of escalation and to seek to negotiate a settlement was dictated by arguments and evidence from within his own administration, and not as a result of congressional pressure. So to some extent he retained his control over policymaking to the end, in spite of the growing opposition. But he paid a high price elsewhere, including the virtual abandonment by Congress of his programs of domestic reform.

Richard Nixon inherited Johnson's willingness to rely on deception and secrecy to assure his dominance over policymaking for Vietnam. But he also inherited the mounting tide of hostility in Congress. Moreover, Nixon contributed to the hostility by his own combative style; and the fact that he was a Republican President facing a Democratic congressional majority further heightened tensions.

Nixon pushed his attempts to dominate national security policy further than any previous President. And he provoked the predictable reaction from Congress—not just the opposition of individuals that Johnson endured, but much broader institutional opposition. This encouraged him to resort even more to secrecy and deception.

At first, the President won general approval for his policy of withdrawing American forces and turning the war over to the South Vietnamese. He accompanied these policies, however, with new escalations designed to throw the enemy off balance, escalations that aroused his opponents at home. For example, the secret bombing of Cambodia, the American-backed ground attacks against Cambodia and Laos, and the mining of North Vietnamese harbors were undertaken without congressional approval, sometimes secretly, and occasionally in defiance of the law.

The congressional opposition began with an attempt to repair past mistakes. In 1971, Congress repealed the Gulf of Tonkin Resolution. But they did not direct the President to end the war; and Nixon, like Johnson, did not believe his authority depended upon the resolution. In any case, Nixon ignored Congress' action. In 1970, Congress prohibited any expenditure to support an American ground attack into Laos or Thailand. A similar enactment in 1971 prohibited the use of ground troops in Cambodia. These acts, however, either came too late to stop

Nixon, or were deliberately—if clandestinely—ignored by him. Broader prohibitions between 1971 and 1973 were defeated in Congress.

In 1973, Congress passed the first of several prohibitions on the expenditure of funds for "combat activity" anywhere in or around Indochina. By 1975, seven such prohibitions had been enacted. Also in 1973, Congress passed the landmark War Powers Resolution, over Nixon's veto. The resolution had two primary purposes.

First, it was intended to prevent future Presidents from entering into armed hostilities without consulting with or even informing Congress. The secret bombing of Cambodia for more than a year during the Nixon administration certainly strengthened Congress' resolve to pursue such an objective. The resolution, therefore, states that the President will "in every possible instance" consult with Congress before sending United States troops into hostilities. If the President does send troops, he must report his reasons for doing so to Congress in writing within forty-eight hours.

Secondly, the resolution was intended to prevent the continuation of a prolonged armed conflict by the President acting alone without the consent of Congress. No doubt, Congress was influenced in this resolve by Lyndon Johnson's prolonged escalation of the Vietnam War acting primarily on his own authority as commander in chief, and only secondarily on the basis of the Gulf of Tonkin Resolution (which, in any case, had been fashioned into a tool of presidential dominance through deception and misuse).

To prevent a similar scenario in the future, the War Powers Resolution requires the President to cease using armed forces in hostilities within sixty days of his report to the Congress if Congress has not declared war or specifically authorized his action by that time. Moreover, Congress may direct the President by a concurrent resolution to remove United States troops from hostilities *before* the sixty-day period elapses if it chooses to do so.

Johnson and Nixon show how far a President can go in ignoring Congress and the public before he is stopped. By appealing to his countrymen's patriotism and by stressing his role as commander in chief, a President may be able to commit the nation to vast and expensive foreign enterprises. But these two presidencies also show how, in the long run, secrecy and deception are no substitute for persuasive power and will generally provoke a bitter congressional reaction with which later Presidents will have to live.

PATTERNS OF PRESIDENTIAL PARTNERSHIP

Presidential dominance of foreign or national-security policy, whether ultimately successful or not, is the exception rather than the rule in presidential-congressional relations. Much more common is the recognition by Presidents that they must concede a substantial share of authority to the legislature. This is particularly true when a President must turn to Congress to appropriate funds, authorize programs, or ratify treaties. In these areas Congress has a constitutionally mandated role; in the absence of pressing military crisis, a President has no alternative but to accept that role and to try to establish a partnership with Congress. If he is to win the support he needs for his policies, he must mobilize his persuasive resources to the full.

Persuading Congress to be an agreeable partner requires more than just presidential messages and appeals for public support—though these are necessary too. The President and his advisers must master the intricate workings of the legislative process, they must understand the myriad and complex pressures that contribute to congressional actions, if they are to deploy their persuasive resources most effectively.

In particular, the President must take into account the nature of the congressional committee system and of the congressional parties. Much of Congress' most important work is done in standing committees, and that is where many battles are won or lost. It will little avail a President to have general support in Congress if the relevant committees are adamantly opposed: Congress usually follows its committees' recommendations. Party loyalty is much less of a factor in Congress, but it cannot be ignored. If the President's own party holds majorities in House and Senate, then appeals to party loyalty may help him win his case. But his party may itself be divided; or it may be the minority. In either case, the President must win support from the opposition party, and must therefore mute his purely partisan appeals. Failure to heed these realities can easily spell defeat.

Public opinion is as important in maintaining this partnership as it is in maintaining dominance. Congress will not long support or share in a policy that the public rejects. The President may benefit from public apathy on an issue: at least there will be few hostile pressures on Congress. But Congress can as easily defy the President as support him in these circumstances. Friendly public opinion is a resource for persuading Congress that a President can seldom afford to ignore.

Two examples will illustrate the way this partnership can succeed or fail.

In 1948, Congress authorized the Marshall Plan to provide huge sums of money for the economic reconstruction of war-devastated Europe. This unprecedented policy was formulated by the Democratic administration of President Truman in 1947. At this time, Republicans held majorities in both houses of Congress, so it was clear that no mere partisan approach would win enough votes. Moreover, with the Democrats themselves split on the issue, there was all the more need for Republican help.

Truman and other senior members of the administration dramatized the plan by emphasizing the importance of Europe to America's security and prosperity, thus appealing across party lines to the bipartisan commitment to Europe of the recent war years. The President also prepared his detailed arguments with great care, establishing three cabinet-level committees to assess the implications of the plan. Congress was thus presented with a proposal that could be vigorously and convincingly defended.

The President's greatest achievement was in winning the support of congressional Republicans. Republicans were asked to tour Europe and see for themselves how urgently economic assistance was needed. In the Senate, Truman worked closely and amicably with the Republican chairman of the Foreign Relations Committee, Senator Vandenberg, making numerous concessions to the senator to win his indispensable support. He agreed to let Vandenberg name the plan's administrator; and he agreed to the senator's demands that the administering agency should be independent of the State Department and run by businessmen rather than diplomats.

As the crucial votes approached, in early 1948, Truman publicly drew attention to Soviet and other Communist advances in Europe, thus successfully harnessing both public and congressional opinion to his policy.

Truman succeeded because he understood and accommodated Congress' institutional sensibilities. He knew he could not have his way by domination, but only through a successful partnership. He needed Congress' willing support, and he deployed considerable skill to get it. This is all the more remarkable since during these same years Truman met considerable opposition in the Republican Congress to his domestic policies.

An example of the breakdown of presidential-congressional partnership is President Woodrow Wilson's attempt in 1919 and 1920 to win Senate ratification for the Treaty of Versailles and the Covenant of the League of Nations. Here too the President could not act alone: the Constitution requires Senate ratification of treaties. Wilson failed, and saw the treaty and the league rejected, because he underestimated his opponents and overestimated himself.

Like Truman, Wilson was a Democratic President facing a Republican-dominated Congress. Many Republicans had been antagonized by the high-handed way he negotiated the treaty in Paris without consulting any senators, and had then virtually demanded that it be ratified. Even this might not have been an insuperable obstacle for the President: straw polls showed that the treaty would pass by the necessary two thirds majority if some changes were made. But, unfortunately for Wilson, Republican opposition was particularly strong in the Foreign Relations Committee, and one of his bitterest opponents, Senator Henry Cabot Lodge, was its chairman. Senate procedures gave Lodge and his fellow committee-members disproportionate influence in the ratification process. Wilson made a difficult problem much worse by refusing to allow the comparatively minor amendments to the treaty that could have won ratification in spite of Lodge's opposition.

In presenting the treaty to the Senate, Wilson adopted a hectoring, arrogant tone. Throughout the ratification process he spoke as though the Senate had no alternative but to approve. He then embarked upon a gruelling nationwide tour to arouse popular support for the treaty. He was well received around the country; but the reception was neither vigorous nor sustained, and it did not translate into new support in the Senate.

Wilson failed to appreciate that so novel a foreign policy as that embodied in the treaty and the league should be presented to Senate and nation only after the most careful political groundwork had been laid. Instead, he antagonized those whose support he needed. He failed to see, as Truman would see three decades later, that the new foreign policy initiative demanded an active partnership with Congress. Instead, Wilson courted failure by placing his faith in his own ability to dominate a situation in which partnership is mandated by the Constitution and by precedent.

CONCLUSIONS

It is important to repeat that patterns of dominance or partnership are not rigidly distinct alternatives. They are each a cluster of tendencies, easily recognizable as distinct in their purest form, but lacking any sharp boundaries between them. Indeed, for most of the time, presidential-congressional relations in foreign policy show features of both patterns. Dominance and partnership, then, are a matter of degree; and they are not necessarily mutually exclusive. Lincoln worked with Congress in some aspects of his war policy; Roosevelt did so even more. Yet in these particular relationships, dominance was the prevailing pattern. Even Johnson and Nixon yielded to Congress a small share of authority in policy for Vietnam. On the other hand, Wilson almost completely undercut his needed partnership with Congress by his inappropriate attempts to dominate. Only Truman's actions, in these examples, show a virtually pure pattern: partnership without dominance.

Certain observations are helpful in attempting to assess the future patterns of presidential-congressional relations in foreign policy and national security. Despite the reassertion of Congress' power in the 1970s, presidential dominance is likely to continue to be the pattern of relating to Congress in times of a perceived military or national security crisis.

Two incidents from the Ford and Carter presidencies are instructive on this point because they occurred *after* Congress had reasserted itself through the War Powers Resolution and other measures. Although the incidents have been described as "rescue missions," it is clear that they were also small-scale military assaults launched in foreign countries.

In May 1975, President Ford ordered a military assault to free thirty-nine United States crewmen believed to be held prisoner by Cambodian Communists aboard the cargo ship *Mayaguez*. All the crewmen were rescued although forty-one servicemen taking part in the mission were killed. In April 1980, President Carter ordered what appears to have been a military assault to free fifty American hostages in Iran. The plan failed in its initial phases of execution and was never carried through.

Although the War Powers Resolution influenced the conduct of Presidents Ford and, to a lesser extent, Carter, it did not deter either of them from assuming dominance over Congress in a situation containing, in their view, an element of military urgency.

Ford consulted with congressional leaders prior to the *Mayaguez* mission only in the limited sense that he told them, rather than asked them, about the mission shortly before it was launched. Unlike Ford, Carter did not inform congressional leaders before launching the hostage rescue mission in Iran.

The fact that both Presidents respected the resolution's requirement of submitting a written report to Congress explaining their actions within forty-eight hours shows that each wished to prevail through presidential persuasion. The respect shown for the reporting requirement, however, in no way indicated that either President regretted asserting his dominance over Congress in the planning and conduct of the rescue missions.

Both Presidents prevailed through persuasion in these two instances. Carter strengthened his persuasive position by appointing Senator Edmund Muskie, the floor manager of the War Powers Resolution when it passed the Senate, as secretary of state to replace Cyrus Vance (who resigned shortly after the hostage rescue attempt failed). Congress generally approved the legality of both rescue missions under the War Powers Resolution, although a few dissenting voices were raised.

Clearly the resolution does not replace presidential dominance with congressional partnership in situations where a military or national security crisis arises. However, the resolution does give Congress a powerful legal and political weapon with which to enter the fray against a dominant President when it *ceases to be persuaded* of the wisdom of his actions as commander in chief.

For example, right before the hostage rescue mission was launched by President Carter, substantial pressure was building in an uneasy Congress for information and consultation concerning major military moves (such as a naval blockade of Iran) which the administration was said to be contemplating. The appointment of Senator Muskie as secretary of state helped to reassure Congress that such a dangerous course of action would not be undertaken without prior consultation with Congress. The reassertion of congressional power in foreign policy matters has significance for another reason. If the military or national security urgency of a foreign-policy issue weighs heavily in determining the degree of presidential dominance (as opposed to partnership) required, then it is especially important that the Congress possess the means, such as the War Powers Resolution provides, to enter prominently into the public debate defining just how urgent a foreign-policy matter is.

In a democratic system, presidential dominance as well as presidential partnership depends finally for its success on the President's ability to persuade Congress. He can neither command nor deceive Congress and be successful over the long run. He may be able to rely, for a while, on congressional apathy or inertia. But if his policies are costly in some measure, as foreign policies usually are, then they will become controversial. Then he will have to resort to skillful persuasion.

The exact mixture of presidential dominance and partnership in the 1980s is impossible to predict with any certainty. It depends on the countless possibilities for interaction between presidential character, political makeup of Congress, public opinion, and major events—all of which remain the great question marks of the coming decade.

Suggested Readings

John C. Donovan, *The Cold Warriors: A Policy-Making Elite.* Lexington, Mass.: Heath, 1974. An analytical discussion of the origins and development of the cold war. Highly critical, but thoughtful.

Paul Y. Hammond, *Cold War and Detente: The American Foreign Policy Process Since 1945.* New York: Harcourt Brace Jovanovich, 1975. A lucid introduction and detailed narrative.

Roger Hilsman, *The Politics of Policy Making in Defense and Foreign Affairs.* New York: Harper and Row, 1971. A brief but authoritative description by a former member of the Kennedy administration.

Henry Kissinger, *The White House Years*. Boston: Little, Brown, 1979. A profound and exhaustive study by the former secretary of state.

Richard M. Pious, *The American Presidency*. New York: Basic Books, 1979. The most recent comprehensive study of the office, with extensive discussion of congressional relations and foreign affairs.

John T. Rourke, "The Future is History: Congress and Foreign Policy," *Presidential Studies Quarterly*, Summer 1979, pp. 275-83. A recent summary and discussion of congressional attempts to curb presidential independence in foreign affairs.

Jonathan Schell, *The Time of Illusion*. New York: Knopf, 1976. A journalist's account of policymaking under Nixon; a thoughtful and provocative study.

Arthur M. Schlesinger, Jr., *The Imperial Presidency*. Boston: Houghton Mifflin, 1973. A comprehensive, historical analysis of the growth of presidential ascendancy in foreign affairs.

Sidney Warren, *The President as World Leader*. New York: McGraw-Hill, 1964. A detailed historical account of foreign and military policy under Presidents from Theodore Roosevelt through Kennedy.

Francis O. Wilcox, *Congress, The Executive, and Foreign Policy*. New York: Harper and Row, 1971. An introductory but scholarly survey.

Aaron Wildavsky, "The Two Presidencies," in Aaron Wildavsky, ed., *The Presidency*. Boston: Little, Brown, 1969, pp. 230-43. A seminal essay that analyzes the differences between foreign and domestic roles of the President.

Harvey G. Zeidenstein, "The Reassertion of Congressional Power: New Curbs on the President," *Political Science Quarterly*, Fall 1978, pp. 393-409. A careful assessment of the impact of recent congressional limits on presidential power, both domestic and foreign.

Chief Justice Warren Burger administers the oath of office to President Nixon during inauguration ceremonies in Washington. *(Religious News Service Photo)*

5

The President and the Federal Courts

Robert Heineman
Alfred University

The dominant theme governing interaction between the presidency and federal courts during this nation's history has been one of cooperation. The confrontations that have occurred have often been highly dramatic and have overshadowed the day-to-day cooperation which characterizes the workings of the two branches of government. Although equal in constitutional theory, in practice the Supreme Court and the lower federal courts are usually no match for presidential power. In wartime crises, for example, confrontations have generally been avoided by the Supreme Court's refusal to challenge the legality of presidential emergency measures.

Nevertheless, dramatic confrontations between the two branches have occurred from time to time. These have established important limits, not only on the power of the federal courts, but on the President's power as well.

THE CONSTITUTIONAL FRAMEWORK

Compared to the treatment of Congress in Article I, the constitutional language covering the presidency in Article II and the federal courts in Article III is sparse. Even less space is given to occasions for interaction between the latter two branches. The President is given the power to make nominations to the courts and the Chief Justice of the Supreme Court is designated a presiding role in impeachment proceedings against a President. Historically, of course, the President's duty to execute the law and the courts' role as final determiners of what the law means have engendered continual intercourse between the two branches.

Presidential Powers. Probably the most fundamental constitutional question attaching to the office of the President is presented by the wording of the opening sentence of Article II. It declares that "The executive Power shall be vested in a President of the United States of America." This wording contrasts markedly with the opening sentence of Article I, which limits Congress to "All legislative Powers herein granted." The fact that the Founding Fathers did not see fit to limit the President to the powers "herein granted" seems to indicate that they believed that the President possessed powers beyond those specifically described in the Constitution.

Sections two and three of Article II briefly list powers and duties of the President. Among the most important of these are his designation as commander in chief of the armed forces, his power to nominate major officeholders, his power to negotiate treaties, and the right to recommend legislation to Congress. Later, in section three, his duties to report "from time to time" to Congress on the state of the union and to "take Care that Laws be faithfully executed" are stated. The veto power of the President is described in section 7 of Article I.

Judicial Powers. The primary constitutional protection given to the federal courts, judicial independence, stands as one of the hallmarks of the American political system. Federal judges retain their offices "during good Behavior" and their salaries may not be reduced while they are in office. They may be removed only by impeachment, a procedure that has been rarely invoked and even more rarely successful. As a consequence of the Constitution's grant of independence, federal judges have been largely immune from political pressures in their decisions and have been able to function as a third policymaking body at the national level. Their power as a policy force in American politics has, of course, been greatly enhanced by their skill in developing an unwritten constitutional tradition that permits them to exercise powers beyond those specifically mentioned in the Constitution.

Chief among the unwritten powers assumed by the Supreme Court has been that of *judicial review,* the voiding of an act of Congress or the President that in the Court's view is contrary to the Constitution. Although this power is exercised infrequently with regard to the Court's coordinate branches at the national level, it constitutes a powerful tool in the policymaking process. Particularly noteworthy is the fact that the Court is nowhere granted the power of judicial review. Its ability to exercise the power stems from the constitutional protection of judicial independence, the esteem that it has been able to maintain in the public mind, and the care with which it has utilized the power.

THE PRESIDENT VERSUS THE COURT

Despite its possession of the power of judicial review, the Supreme Court remains subordinate to the power of the presidency in most important respects. The President has at his disposal the forces for action. He can act to avert a crisis; he can act to precipitate one; and he can act to resolve one. The Court is dependent on the initiative of others for its effectiveness as a policymaking body. Cases must be brought before it; only in the act of deciding these cases can it search out policy issues to resolve. Furthermore, it must rely on the willingness of the executive branch in many instances for implementation of its decisions. Generally, the Court has demonstrated a marked aversion to direct confrontations with Presidents who have been in a position to undermine the status of the Court simply by ignoring its decisions. During wartime, especially, the Court has deemed it wiser to defer to executive powers when individual liberties have been curtailed. During the Vietnam War, it consistently refused to grant standing to individuals and organizations who sought to have the federal courts examine the legality of that war.

An occasion when the Court temporarily lost its sensitivity to the power of a politically popular and powerful President was provided by the New Deal Court. President Franklin D. Roosevelt believed that the severity of the Great Depression called for dramatic economic action by the national government. Unfortunately for the President a majority of the Supreme Court opposed government economic intervention and through the exercise of judicial review began to dismantle much of his New Deal program. With his reelection in 1936 by a resounding margin, President Roosevelt determined to move against the Supreme Court.

Seizing on the fact that six of the nine justices were past seventy, FDR proposed that for every justice past seventy the President be empowered to appoint an additional justice, with the size of the Court limited to fifteen. The President's proposal was perfectly legal; Congress clearly has power over the size of the Court.

Although there was strong opposition to FDR's initiative in Congress, the Court did not seek a confrontation with the President. Rather, it acted to remedy the causes behind his proposal. With what Professor Edward S. Corwin termed "the switch in time that saved nine," the Court began to uphold the constitutionality of the economic and social legislation of the New Deal. Only then, did Congress kill the President's "Court packing" plan. The President's effort had served its purpose, for since its "switch" the Court has virtually removed itself as a constitutional check on economic and social policy.

President Nixon's clash with the Burger Court in the celebrated tapes case occurred in a context significantly different from that of 1937, but the outcome again indicates the importance of public pressure in the relations between the Court and the President. Unlike the case with FDR, President Nixon's popularity was at a low ebb at the time that *U.S.* v *Nixon* 418 US 683 (1974) was decided. Additionally, he faced active impeachment proceedings in the House of Representatives. Thus, the Court was in a fairly powerful position when in a unanimous opinion it directly ordered the President to act. With no effective source of support, he had little choice but to release the tapes, an act that rather quickly led to his resignation.

The Uneasy Partnership: Presidential Implementation of Court Decisions

The presidential tapes case presented another among a number of recent instances when Presidents have evidenced a willingness to resist Court decisions. In this instance President Nixon noted that he would need a clear, definitive decision on the issue, apparently hinting that he might not comply unless all the justices ruled that he must. The unanimous opinion of the eight participating justices*, however, left him with no basis for

---

*Justice Rehnquist did not participate.

questioning the law enunciated by the Court. The unified front presented by the Court in this instance avoided further difficulties for it. But there are indications that underlying social forces in the nation have weakened the public's expectation that a President must dutifully follow Court decisions.

In its 1954 refusal to condone segregation by race in the public schools, the Court initiated two decades of tension between itself and those public officials who were opposed to implementing the 1954 desegregation decision. The issue of racial equality in the public schools became particularly volatile as the Court began to consider problems in the North and West as well as the South and as politicians such as Governor Wallace emerged to lead public dissatisfaction. The Burger Court in *Swann* v. *Charlotte-Mecklenburg* 402 US 1 (1971) suggested that busing was one legitimate means for bringing racial balance to school districts. As lower federal courts began to impose busing plans, public feeling was raised to a fever pitch. In the face of increasing support for the Wallace effort throughout the country, the Nixon administration felt compelled to act to weaken the power of the federal courts in the area of busing. In the aftermath of the Charlotte-Mecklenburg decision President Nixon had followed clear Court decisions but had ordered his administration to go no further than absolutely necessary in obeying lower federal court orders. By March of 1972, he concluded that more drastic action was needed and on March 16 in a national television address he proposed that Congress impose a moratorium on federal court busing decisions by removing temporarily jurisdiction over these cases from the federal courts.

The removal of Governor Wallace from active campaigning due to the injuries suffered when he was wounded tended to blunt the effectiveness of the antibusing forces and the President's proposal died in Congress. Nonetheless it raises interesting constitutional questions. Nixon's approach had a semblance of legality about it in that Congress has control over the jurisdiction of the lower federal courts. However, he was suggesting using a congressional statute to weaken a Court interpretation of the Constitution. It is difficult to see how the justices would have allowed a statute to stand which was aimed at diluting the rights proclaimed by their interpretation of the Constitution.

PRESIDENTIAL POWER AS FRAMED
BY THE SUPREME COURT

In his capability for action, the President has a significant advantage over Congress and the federal courts. In a crisis the President is expected to act because he is the only source of effective action at the national level. Furthermore, through the resources at his disposal, he can maneuver Congress into a position where it has little choice but to support him. When President Ford acted forcefully and quickly to recover the Mayaguez from its Cambodian captors in May of 1975, Congress found itself in just such a position.

The practical power of the President to act increases the constitutional difficulties raised by the ambiguity of the opening statement in Article II. As was pointed out earlier, the President's powers included in that article are not as clearly anchored to the words of the Constitution as are the powers of Congress. This area of *inherent* executive power to act without direct authorization from the Constitution or from Congress constitutes what is termed presidential prerogative. Its boundaries remain the subject of controversy. Given its sensitivity to presidential power, the Supreme Court has only occasionally attempted to explore the limits of presidential prerogative. There is, therefore, no clear series of Court decisions defining prerogative power. It is obvious, however, that the Court has granted the President his greatest sweep of power during wartime and that it has generally been sympathetic to the broad exercise of power in the area of foreign affairs.

Prerogative in Wartime and in Foreign Affairs. The Court's deference to the President's role as commander in chief during wartime has paralleled some of the most serious executive abuses of individual liberties in this nation's history. One of the greatest excesses in this respect was the Roosevelt administration's treatment of the West Coast Japanese and Japanese-Americans during WWII. After the attack on Pearl Harbor, these people, many of whom were American citizens, were forcibly moved to inland camps where they were held for most of the war. Despite the absence of any semblance of due process, Justice Black, one of the more liberal justices and a man who would later write to limit presidential power severely, upheld the government's action in the case of *Korematsu* v. *U.S.* 323 US 214 (1944). His opinion over-

rode the bitter dissent of Justice Murphy, who declared that the
relocation program had gone "over 'the very brink of constitutional power' " and had fallen "into the ugly abyss of racism."

Examination of Supreme Court treatment of presidential
power in foreign affairs reveals that in this area the Court has
rather consistently taken the position that the President is entitled to a degree of prerogative power. Speaking for the Court
in *U.S.* v. *Curtiss-Wright Export Corporation* 299 US 304 (1936)
Justice Sutherland declared that the President must be allowed
flexibility when speaking and acting for the nation internationally. He noted:

> . . .In this vast external realm, with its important, compli-
> cated, delicate and manifold problems, the president alone
> has the power to speak or listen as a representative of the
> nation. . . . [C] ongressional legislation. . .must often accord
> to the president a degree of discretion and freedom from
> statutory restriction which would not be admissible were
> domestic affairs alone involved.

The *Curtiss-Wright* decision lends weight to the view that
the President's prerogative power is broader in foreign affairs than
in domestic affairs. However, the decision did not make clear just
what the President's inherent powers in foreign affairs were.

Presidents themselves have expressed different opinions
about their prerogative powers. Theodore Roosevelt contended
that his power in both foreign and domestic affairs was quite
broad. As "steward" of the nation's welfare, he believed he could
take any action not forbidden by the Constitution or by Congress.
Roosevelt's successor, Taft, took a restrictive view of presidential
power. He maintained that if Congress or the Constitution did
not authorize him to act, he could not do so, a position that virtually eliminated the prerogative power of the President. Naturally, Presidents have tended to favor Roosevelt's interpretation of
presidential power and in the area of foreign policy, the Court has
tended to agree. However, where domestic activities have been
concerned, the Supreme Court has come down much closer to
Taft's position.

Prerogative in Domestic Affairs. The most complete recent statement about the prerogative power of the President in domestic
matters was made in the Court's response to President Truman's
seizure of the steel mills during the Korean War. In *Youngstown
Sheet & Tube* v. *Sawyer* 343 US 579 (1952) the Court in a 6-3

decision held that President Truman had exceeded his powers. Justice Black's opinion for the Court reflected President Taft's restrictive view of presidential prerogative. Congress, said Black, has exclusive power to legislate and the President is limited by the Constitution "...to the recommending of laws that he thinks wise and the vetoing of laws he thinks bad. ...." Each of the five concurring justices disagreed with Black's restrictive view and with varying degrees of leeway would have granted the President inherent power to act in emergency situations. All agreed, however, that in this instance President Truman had overstepped constitutional limits by his refusal to utilize the Taft-Hartley Act of 1947, in which Congress had provided guidelines for settling this kind of labor dispute. The three dissenting justices would have gone even further and allowed the steel mill seizure despite the existence of the Taft-Hartley Act. It seems probable, then, that without the existence of the Taft-Hartley Act, President Truman's action would have commanded the support of a majority of the Supreme Court. The considerable support among the justices for the President's prerogative power was obscured both by the Taft-Hartley Act and by Justice Black's restrictive opinion for the Court. Therefore, while restricting President Truman in the case at hand, the Youngstown decision left unclear the larger question of the scope of the President's prerogative power in domestic affairs.

Executive Privilege and Watergate. The most recent Court decisions dealing with presidential prerogative have involved the privacy that should be accorded a President's communications and conversations. These decisions may be limited in their general applicability because they stem from the hopefully unique circumstances surrounding the Watergate Affair. President Nixon received little sympathy from the Burger Court in these decisions and if they are to serve as precedents for later Presidents, they could prove to be quite restrictive.

The first Supreme Court case dealing with President Nixon's claims of presidential or *executive privilege* resulted from his refusal to release tape recordings of his conversations. The Court through Chief Justice Burger rejected decisively the President's claim that he was entitled to total confidentiality in his conversations. The Court took the position that the tapes were needed as evidence in criminal proceedings against the President's former aides and that the President could not use his claim of privilege to undermine the integrity of the judicial process. Subsequent to the *U.S.* v. *Nixon* decision, President Nixon entered into an agreement with the General Services Administration for storage of his documents and tapes. The agreement provided also for the eventual destruction of the tapes. Congress responded with the Preservation of Presidential Recordings and Materials Act of 1974, which required that these materials be turned over to the GSA for screening and storage. In *Nixon* v. *Administrator of General Services,* 433 US 425 (1977), the Court in a 7-2 decision upheld the constitutionality of the act, citing the unusual circumstances surrounding the Nixon resignation.

The fact that Nixon was unable to protect private conversations taped in the White House from inspection by the federal courts, and eventually by Congress and the general public, could weaken future Presidents. The Nixon cases could be used as precedents to force a President to relinquish records of private White House conversations dealing with general domestic policy matters.

The Supreme Court's reasoning in these cases, however, does little to encourage this development. In *U.S.* v. *Nixon,* the Court emphasized that the tapes to be relinquished contained evidence pertinent to a criminal prosecution. In the absence of such a compelling circumstance, the *Nixon* case would lose much of its force as a legal precedent to be used against a future President's claim of executive privilege.

Perhaps more important, the Supreme Court stated more clearly than ever before that executive privilege is a legitimate power of the President, especially where sensitive foreign policy and national security matters are concerned. It may well be, therefore, that although the Supreme Court rejected Nixon's claim of executive privilege in this particular case, the decision will strengthen rather than weaken the ability of future Presidents to make such a claim stand up in the federal courts.

THE PRESIDENT AND CONGRESS: JUDICIAL INTERVENTION IN THE BALANCE OF POWER

Presidential Powers of Appointment and Removal. The Constitution distinguishes between the President's power to *appoint* officers in the executive branch and Congress' power to *create* these offices. The Supreme Court has recently reaffirmed the importance of this distinction. In *Buckley* v. *Valeo* 424 US 1 (1976) the Court was unanimous in its position that congressional appointments to the Federal Election Commission violated the President's powers to appoint executive officers. Congress has no power to appoint officers engaged in essentially nonlegislative functions.

The more important issue in terms of presidential influence on policy direction has been that dealing with the President's power of removal. Unfortunately, except for its treatment of impeachment, the Constitution is silent on the question of who has the power to remove executive officers.

In the twentieth century the President's power of removal was stated in very broad terms by Chief Justice William Howard Taft in *Myers* v. *U.S.* 272 US 52 (1926). He argued that all non-civil service executive officers appointed by the President were subject to dismissal by the President alone. Taft asserted that the President could not be bound by any restrictions on removal that Congress may have attempted to impose. However, later Supreme Court decisions have restricted the President's removal power with regard to those officials serving on independent regulatory agencies.

These agencies have never been viewed as being strictly executive in nature and were created by Congress to be largely independent of the President's control. The Court in *Humphrey's Executor* v. *U.S.* 295 US 602 (1935) sharply limited the President's power to dismiss officials serving on such agencies. The protection that the courts have given members of independent regulatory agencies such as the Federal Trade Commission has strengthened congressional control over these agencies and helped to weaken presidential direction of policy. In practice, the areas of economic policy controlled by these agencies are heavily influenced by congressional leaders who often assume positions competitive with those of the President.

Additionally, it is important to note that the Court has become increasingly critical of the use of political patronage considerations for determining job tenure at the local level of government. In recent years the Court has consistently blocked attempts by elected local officials to remove subordinates of a different political persuasion in order to replace them with individuals from their party.* Most recently, in *Branti* v. *Finkel* 48 USLW 4331 (1980), it held that before a person could be dismissed for partisan political reasons his or her supervisor must show that party affiliation is "an appropriate requirement" for the "effective performance" of the job involved.

In this decision the Court was dealing with the relatively small number of government jobs not already protected from partisan manipulation by federal and state civil service laws. Many students of politics believe that governmental leaders, including the President, need this remaining pool of patronage positions in order to be able to provide meaningful direction and implementation of policy. While it is true that the immediate impact of the *Branti* decision was limited to local level politics, the principle of the case seems to apply also to presidential patronage appointments.

At present, the patronage positions that the President can use to exert his personal influence over the bureaucracy, the Congress, or his political party comprise less than 1 percent of all federal employees. If the federal courts follow the logic of their current decisions and extend the principle of the *Branti* decision to this limited number of executive non-civil service positions, the President's ability to provide leadership and to exert policy influence at the national level would quite probably be weakened even further.

Presidential Power over Federal Spending and Programs. When Congress has not been able to act, groups sympathetic to programs enacted by it have turned to the federal courts for relief from presidential incursions. The impoundment and Office of Economic Opportunity cases demonstrate the willingness of the courts to act against a President.

The Impoundment Controversy. When a President has impounded funds, it means essentially that he has refused to spend monies appropriated by Congress. Presidents previous to the Nixon administration had occasionally impounded funds, but President Nixon forced a legal test of the issues involved in impoundment because of his extensive use of the technique. In 1973 his impoundment actions were challenged in numerous suits filed in the lower federal courts. The President argued that there was a

---

*See *Elrod* v. *Burns* 427 US 347 (1976).

need to act to hold inflation in check and relied on several statutes that gave him general responsibility for economic policy. The courts, however, were not sympathetic to the Nixon position. With but few exceptions, they took the position that the constitutional provision requiring the President to see that the "laws are faithfully executed" prevented him from refusing to spend monies duly appropriated by congressional statute.

The impoundment controversy was temporarily resolved by the passage of the Budget Impoundment and Control Act of 1974, which specified the conditions under which a President could refuse to spend monies appropriated by Congress. The Ford administration promptly interpreted the act as recognizing that the President had at least limited impoundment authority, an interpretation that was supported by House leaders and the General Accounting Office but hotly disputed by liberal Senate leaders. Nonetheless, the Ford administration was careful to avoid the wholesale impoundments attempted by its predecessor and the Carter administration also declined to test the limits of the act.

The Attack on the Office of Economic Opportunity. At the same time that he was challenging Congress with the impoundment of funds, President Nixon boldly assaulted the Office of Economic Opportunity, the flagship agency of the previous administration's "war on poverty." Congress had authorized the existence of OEO through fiscal 1974, or June 30, 1974, but President Nixon refused to request funds for its operation during that last year. He then appointed Howard Phillips acting director of the agency for the purpose of dismantling it. Alarmed by the President's actions, clientele of the OEO's programs sued to stop them in Federal District Court and were rewarded with a favorable decision. U.S. District Judge William Jones ordered Acting Director Phillips to halt his efforts to dismantle the agency. He held that the President could not abolish an agency that still had congressional authorization to exist and that reorganization of an agency must proceed through the reorganization process provided by congressional statute. The administration did not appeal Judge Jones' decision, apparently because it feared that an unfavorable decision by a higher court would jeopardize the impoundment cases then pending. Congress appropriated funds for another year, after which the Ford administration proceeded to disperse the various agency programs with the acquiescence of Congress.

PRESIDENTIAL POWER IN FOREIGN AFFAIRS: LEADERSHIP UNDER CHALLENGE

In the area of foreign policy the powers of the President remain broad, despite increasing challenges, because of the need, as noted in the *Curtiss-Wright* decision, for someone to speak and act for the nation. The tendency of the Court to support presidential power in this area can be seen in its decisions relating to international agreements.

The Power to Make International Agreements. The most formal approach to international agreements is the negotiation of treaties, which require the approval of two thirds of the Senate. It is established practice that the President negotiates treaties and the Senate ratifies or rejects them. Treaties are important in terms of the nation's international obligations but are also important domestically because they, along with federal statutes and the Constitution, are the supreme law of the land.

Presidents may also enter into international agreements without using the treaty process. This approach seems justified by Article I, section 10, clause 3 of the Constitution which uses language indicating that international agreements other than treaties are possible. Presidential agreements with other nations that have not been ratified as treaties are called executive agreements. Modern Presidents clearly prefer executive agreements to the more cumbersome treaty ratification process. Between 1971 and 1977, for example, Presidents concluded more than eighteen executive agreements for every treaty ratified during that period. (Robert Di Clerico, *The American President,* Prentice-Hall, 1979, p. 47)

Most of these agreements, however, have been made pursuant to congressional authorization and have rarely raised fundamental constitutional issues. The areas of controversy focus on those agreements made without congressional authorization.

The Supreme Court has supported presidential power by holding that executive agreements have the same force in domestic law as treaties, and they are, of course, binding internationally. The availability of the executive agreement technique raises the possibility that a President may choose to enter into important foreign commitments without submitting them to two-thirds approval of the Senate. In many instances an executive agreement requires congressional implementation to be effective, but it may be easier to achieve simple majorities in both houses of Congress than to obtain a two-thirds majority in the Senate. Congressional concern about the possibility of secret executive agreements during the latter stages of the Vietnam War led to several efforts to limit the President in this respect. The result was Public Law 92-404, which requires the President to inform Congress of any foreign agreement within sixty days of its becoming effective. Stronger efforts to limit presidential flexibility in this area failed, indicating continuing congressional reservations about tying a President's hands too severely in foreign policy.

The Power to Break International Agreements: The Goldwater Challenge on Taiwan. President Carter's declaration that he would terminate the United States defense treaty with Taiwan at the end of 1979 provoked an instance of congressional-court interaction that may be indicative of future efforts to limit the Chief Executive. Senator Goldwater and a number of current and former congressmen immediately sued in federal court claiming that President Carter could not take such action without Senate approval. U.S. District Court Judge Oliver Gasch was obviously sympathetic to Goldwater's original suit but held that without any indication of congressional disapproval Goldwater had no basis for suit. Within hours of Judge Gasch's dismissal of the suit, the Senate passed a resolution declaring it to be the sense of the Senate that the President could not terminate any mutual defense treaty without its approval. Goldwater reinstituted his suit and Judge Gasch then held that the President could not terminate the treaty with Taiwan without Senate approval or approval by simple majorities in both houses of Congress. The Carter administration refused to ask for Senate approval of its action and appealed Judge Gasch's ruling to the U.S. Circuit Court of Appeals, where it won a reversal. The Supreme Court without opinion ordered the suit dismissed. Thus, President Carter's decision remained in force.

The action by Goldwater and his colleagues parallels the efforts of those fighting President Nixon's impoundment actions and his attempt to abolish the Office of Economic Opportunity. In each instance a small group asked the federal courts to stop the President's actions on the grounds that he had exceeded his authority and was infringing on the authority of Congress.

THE PRESIDENT AND THE FEDERAL JUDGES:
THE POWER OF APPOINTMENT

Through wise selection of federal judges a President can ensure that his policy preferences will have representation at the national level long after he has taken his last official ride down Pennsylvania Avenue. Presidents are, of course, limited by the number of vacancies that occur during their terms in office and by the need for Senate approval.

The Politics of Judicial Appointment. An individual's positions on the important policy issues of the day and his or her party affiliation are the most important political considerations that enter into a President's choice of a judicial nominee.

It is understandable that Presidents prefer to have judges who are sympathetic to their views on national issues. All Presidents take this factor into consideration, but the actions of Presidents Franklin Roosevelt and Nixon stand out in this respect because of the clear and fundamental changes that their appointments made on the Supreme Court. Although he was frustrated in his attempt to enlarge the Court, FDR's careful attention to the ideological orientations of those he appointed to the Court soon resulted in a substantial Court majority sympathetic to his policies. All of the four individuals appointed by President Roosevelt to the Court previous to 1940 had worked in the New Deal administration or had closely identified themselves with its goals. Similarly, President Nixon argued that the expansionist tendencies of the Warren Court must be halted through the appointment of "strict constructionists" of the Constitution to the Court. Accordingly, his four appointments to the Court were all men who could be expected to take more restrictive positions on issues in the areas of civil rights and liberties. And while it has not overturned any of the Warren Court's major advances, the Burger Court has slowed the pace of change.

From the Truman administration through the middle of President Carter's first term, no President with the exception of President Ford, who appointed 79 percent Republicans at the district court level, has chosen more than 10 percent of his appointments to the lower federal courts from outside of his party. Appointments to the Supreme Court have also been marked by a pattern of political partisanship on the part of Presidents. President Carter's appointments to the federal courts have been significantly more diversified than those of his predecessors in that they have reflected the increasing political power of minorities and women. The percentage of women appointed by him to the district court level is much higher than that of Presidents Ford, Nixon, or Johnson, and 25 percent of his first twelve appointments to the Court of Appeals were black. Despite the sociological diversity which characterized President Carter's judicial appointments, it is clear that party affiliation remained an important consideration in his choices. In fact appointments from his party to the district courts constitute a higher percentage of the total appointments at this level than that produced by any of his three most recent predecessors.

The Supreme Court. Examination of appointments to the Supreme Court reveals that Presidents usually consider geographic diversity an important element on the Court. In the past the Northeast has been heavily represented on the Court, a situation that reflected the distribution of political power in the country. Most recently the Nixon and Ford appointments to the Court have changed this imbalance and accorded more representation to the Midwest, South, and West. The current Court thus mirrors the shift in political power away from the Northeast.

Religion has also received attention in appointments to the Court, although today it is difficult to say how important it continues to be. The appointment of Louis D. Brandeis in 1916 began the tradition that one seat on the Court would remain Jewish. The tradition ended in 1969 when President Nixon chose not to replace Justice Abe Fortas, who had resigned, with another Jewish justice. For a number of years there was also a "Catholic" seat on the Court. That tradition was broken by President Truman, although presently Justice William J. Brennan, a Catholic, may represent a renewal of that tradition.

President Johnson sought to extend the representativeness of the Court by his appointment of the first black justice, Thurgood Marshall. Johnson undoubtedly saw this appointment as emphasizing his support for the civil rights movement and he was careful to select a person with extensive legal experience. Whether black representation will continue on the Court after Justice Marshall leaves will depend on the priorities of the President at the time.

One factor that almost certainly will have to be given consideration by Presidents of the next decade is that of the sex of their appointees. The Supreme Court has remained an all-male institution throughout its history, but as women attorneys become more numerous and attain more positions of power in the government and the political parties, this distinction will become politically untenable. It is to be expected also that the greater number of sexual discrimination cases coming before the Court will increase public pressure for female appointments.

Consideration of Prior Judicial Experience. Some Presidents have maintained that only persons who have actually served as judges should be appointed to the Supreme Court. President Eisenhower expressed this view. Except for his appointment of Earl Warren to the Chief Justiceship—an appointment viewed as a reward for Warren's support of Eisenhower's 1952 presidential bid—President Eisenhower appointed only judges to the Court. Even Brennan, a Democrat appointed by him to show that he was not narrowly partisan, was a sitting judge. Presidents Nixon and Ford generally followed their Republican predecessor's lead in this respect. Although Republican Presidents have argued that judicial experience is an important criterion for appointment to the Court, it is also quite likely that they feel much more secure appointing an individual who has already rendered in a judicial capacity decisions basically compatible with their views. Once an individual has become a judge, there is no reason to believe that elevation to the Supreme Court will substantially change the views that he has already expressed under the protection of judicial independence.

Democratic Presidents have generally not appointed sitting judges to the Court, yet the quality of the justices obtained under this approach seems to be the equivalent of that obtained by Republican Presidents. In terms of producing some predictability in judicial behavior on the Supreme Court a strong case can be made for appointing sitting judges. But in terms of obtaining high quality justices, prior judicial experience alone does not appear to be of more importance than a range of other considerations.

Confirmation by the Senate. The Constitution requires that the Senate confirm all presidential nominees to the Supreme Court and to the lower federal courts. Until the Johnson administration only one Supreme Court nominee in the twentieth century had been defeated by the Senate. The break with this tradition began with President Johnson's attempt to elevate his friend, Justice Fortas, to the position of Chief Justice. Led by Senator Robert Griffin of Michigan, a coalition of Republicans and southern Democrats successfully filibustered against the nomination and raised so much controversy regarding Justice Fortas that he resigned from the Court. In retrospect the incident marked the end of automatic Senate ratification of presidential nominations to the Court.

President Nixon also reaped some of the effects of the more aggressive Senate attitude toward Supreme Court nominations. His nomination of Warren Burger to the Chief Justiceship was ratified without difficulty. But his nomination of Judge Clement Haynsworth from South Carolina to fill a seat on the Court was defeated in large part because senators found Judge Haynsworth's lower court decisions on civil rights and labor questions unpalatable. Nixon responded by nominating another Southern judge, George Carswell, whose background, especially in civil rights, was also unacceptable to a majority of the Senate. Finally, the President turned to Judge Harry Blackmun of Minnesota, who was approved.

It is clear that the actions of the Senate in the Johnson and Nixon administrations provide recent precedent for further rejections of presidential nominees and this possibility must be taken into consideration by any President making nominations to the Court in the near future. Moreover, Nixon's experience demonstrates that if a President can read a sitting judge's record, so also can the Senate.

Appointments to the Lower Federal Courts. Lower federal court judgeships are the prize political patronage plums of national politics. For this reason individual senators, through the custom of "senatorial courtesy," have assumed the power to determine who shall receive these appointments. Under the unwritten rules of senatorial courtesy, a President must clear his judicial nomination with the senator or senators of his party from the state involved. If he does not, the Senate will reject the nomination. The Senate stands together on this issue because no senator wants a President handing out patronage plums to rival factions within the party in his or her state. If there is no senator of the President's party from a state, then, of course, a President has more flexibility in making an appointment.

During his campaign for the presidency, Carter threatened to end the Senate's control over judicial patronage by promising to choose federal judges on a merit basis. However, as President, the best he could do in this respect was to establish a U.S. Circuit Judge Nominating Committee that would recommend nominees for U.S. Circuit Court vacancies. Furthermore, senators were assured that they would have input into this process. On the district court level, he met with complete defeat in his efforts to institute a merit approach. In the 1978 bill creating additional district court judgeships, the Senate insisted on its traditional rights and in the final version of the bill retained control over the 117 new patronage plums.

A COMMENT ON THE FUTURE

From the evidence now available, it would appear that judicial treatment of presidential actions in the 1980s will depend heavily on the contexts in which these actions are challenged in the courts. Certainly, the federal courts in the 1970s have produced no clear or consistent definition of presidential power. Generally, the Supreme Court has been willing to uphold presidential actions. Where it has not during the past decade, as in the Nixon tapes cases, it has carefully based its decisions on narrow issues and particular, perhaps unique, circumstances. In the area of national security it has continued a position of deference to the President's judgment. Most importantly, the federal courts have not restated the restrictions on presidential power in the narrow terms used by Justice Black in the steel seizure case.

On the other hand, the judicial reaction to Nixon's assault on established federal programs and to Senator Goldwater's challenge on the Taiwan treaty issue has left a legacy of lower court decisions that are unsympathetic to presidential power and could be used to mount challenges to future Chief Executives. Moreover, the Supreme Court in 1980 came very close to challenging the President's power to make patronage appointments in the few remaining federal jobs not protected by the Civil Service Act.

In view of the uncertain legacy left by the federal judiciary in the 1970s, the judicial treatment of presidential power in the 1980s is likely to be heavily influenced by the unfolding of events. If in the coming decade the international situation or the economy deteriorate seriously, the federal courts will probably be supportive of executive power. Alternatively, a decade of relative peace and stability could strengthen the position of those forces wishing to use the federal courts to advance their claims against the presidency.

Suggested Readings

Abraham, Henry J. *Justices and Presidents: A Political History of Appointments to the Supreme Court.* Baltimore: Penguin Books, 1975. This historical treatment of presidential appointments to the Supreme Court begins with Washington and runs through the Nixon administration. Abraham spends time on the political considerations entering into the selection of justices and deals briefly with the performance of each as a member of the Court. The twentieth century receives more treatment than the nineteenth and the Nixon and Johnson administrations are considered in detail. There is also a chapter summarizing the procedural issues involved in appointment to the Court.

Ball, Howard. *Courts and Politics: The Federal Judicial System.* Englewood Cliffs: Prentice-Hall, 1980. Ball provides a good overview of the federal court system that is written in an interesting, clear manner. Unlike many treatments of the judicial process, this book contains considerable material on the lower federal courts. The case studies are useful illustrations of how the federal courts operate. Those dealing with appointments under the Johnson, Nixon, and Carter administrations give excellent insights into how politics enters into the relations between the presidency and the court system at all levels.

Corwin, Edward S. *The President: Office and Powers, 1787-1957.* New York: New York University Press, 1957. Although it is now dated, this book remains one of the classic treatments of the presidency. It is well written and extensively documented. Corwin gives a historical perspective on presidential powers and much of his treatment is in terms of constitutional and court definitions of these powers. For background on many of the current issues involving the presidency, this is a good place to begin.

Schwartz, Bernard. *The Powers of the President.* Volume two of *The Powers of Government.* New York: Macmillan, 1963. This is one volume of Schwartz's five-volume *A Commentary on the Constitution of the United States.* Schwartz provides a thorough examination of the Supreme Court's treatment of presidential powers. He has separate chapters on the President's powers in foreign affairs and his war powers. The work is extensively documented and Schwartz makes a commendable effort at synthesizing Court rulings into coherent explanations of presidential powers.

Scigliano, Robert. *The Supreme Court and the Presidency.* New York: Free Press, 1971. Scigliano examines the relations between the presidency and the Court from the intentions of the Founding Fathers through the Lyndon Johnson administration. He discusses the important issues that exist between the two branches including the question of a President's obligation to obey a Court decision. Also included is useful material on the Justice Department's role in bringing cases before the Court. Scigliano's general thesis is that the courts and the President have usually worked in tandem to limit Congress.

Woodward, Bob and Scott Armstrong. *The Brethren: Inside the Supreme Court.* New York: Simon and Schuster, 1979. This book by two journalists is an extensive look inside the Supreme Court under Chief Justice Burger. It is based on interviews and internal Court communications. Probably too much effort is spent trying to discredit Chief Justice Burger and serious questions have been raised about the accuracy of some of the reconstructed conversations. Nonetheless, the glimpses into the inner Court are fascinating and there are ample examples of the Court's sensitivity to the presidency and politics.

DATE DUE
